COOKING THE

Three Dog Bakery Way

COOKING THE
Three Dog Bakery Way

Mark Beckloff and Dan Dye

Illustrations by Meg Cundiff

○ BROADWAY BOOKS, NEW YORK ○

BROADWAY

PRINTED IN THE UNITED STATES OF AMERICA

BROADWAY BOOKS and its logo, a letter B bisected on the diagonal, are trademarks of Random House, Inc. Visit our website at www.broadwaybooks.com

First edition published 2005

Book design by rlf design

Library of Congress Cataloging-in-Publication Data
Beckloff, Mark.
Cooking the Three Dog Bakery Way / Mark Beckloff and Dan Dye.
        p.   cm.
1. Dogs—Food—Recipes.   2. Three Dog Bakery (Kansas City, Mo.)
        I. Dye, Dan.   II. Title.
SF427.4.B424 2005
636.7'085—dc22
2004061780

ISBN 0-7679-1819-3

1 3 5 7 9 10 8 6 4 2

To Sarah, Dottie, and Gracie, our "girls,"

who were the real brains behind the bakery

and the true inspiration for it all

He deserves paradise who makes
his companions laugh.

—*The Koran*

The greatness of a nation and its
moral progress can be judged by the
way its animals are treated.

—*Mohandas Gandhi, Indian leader*

I don't believe in the concept of hell,
but if I did, I would think of it as filled with
people who were cruel to animals.

—*Gary Larson, cartoonist*

Contents

Foreword

Cooking the Three Dog Bakery Way is a delightful addition to the library of those interested in cooking snacks and occasional full meals for canine family members. The recipes contain only natural and wholesome ingredients as explained in the first chapter, "Our Pantry—and Yours," which by itself is valuable information. In addition to a large complement of dog-friendly and tasty recipes for appetizers, entrees, and desserts, the text is replete with tips, facts, and advice about dogs, e.g., preventing obesity, recognizing the signs of cancer, care of the older dog, and so on. The authors, Mark and Dan, are masters, not only as canine chefs but also in presenting their recipes and other important information in an easy-to-read and most entertaining fashion.

Francis A. Kallfelz, DVM, PhD
James Law Professor of Veterinary Nutrition
College of Veterinary Medicine, Cornell University

Acknowledgments

We'd like to nuzzle up to the following people for their help in pulling this project together:

Tanya McKinnon, our literary agent at Mary Evans, Inc., for her guidance, good energy, and wit. Jennifer Josephy, our wonderful, steely-eyed editor, who guided this book to its completion, correcting our grammar and spelling every inch of the way. Richard Simon, our hilarious, talented, and much-loved friend, who listens and inspires. And a big tail wag to the entire dog-loving staff at Three Dog Bakery—bakers, packagers, administrative, management, and retail bakeries—who work so hard to make the brand shine.

Special pawshakes to Kathy Warren, VP merchandising; Bonnie Yarmo, our KC bakery manager; Patrick Ramsey, Executive Pastry Chef; Thomas Hudson, Director, Quality Control; Mark Muchmore, Personal Chef; and Dr. Mark Finke, for their help with the recipes in this book.

Tummy rubs to you all.

COOKING THE

Three Dog Bakery Way

$\mathcal{I}$ntro**dog***tion*

A *very long time ago* (*specifically,* three epochs, two eons, and half an era, at around six-thirty in the morning), a long-tailed and bushy-coated animal called *Cynodictis* started his slo-o-o-ow evolution through a wolfish foreparent (*Canis lupus pallipes,* or "wolf-dog with covered paws") into *Canis familiaris*—better known as man's best friend. In the millennia since then, dogs have kept us warm at night, protected our homes, warded off untold dangers, and saved our lives—and all without a thought in their furry heads about repayment for services rendered.

Don't you think they deserve—at the very *least*—a tray of fresh-baked SnickerPoodles?

If you do, then welcome to Three Dog Bakery—the world's very first, *bone*-i-fide, four-paw bakery . . . *for dogs!* Three Dog Bakery is a canine confectionery, a pooch patisserie, a mecca for mutts—where dogs go to see and be seen, sniff and be sniffed, nibble and be nibbled. Our unique bakeries are scattered across the world, and every one of them is full of fresh foods, de*leash*ous treats, fun, fur, cold noses, and tail-wagging galore.

We Are the World's *Original* Bakery for Dogs

Let us tell you about what we do, just in case your dog has not been lucky enough to visit one of our bakeries (or to have you fetch something for him or her). Our bakeries give *"baked from scratch"* a whole new meaning. We are a chain of full-service, full-line, fully working bakeries—and it's all for dogs! Where else on earth can a pooch go for such *paw*-rennial favorites as PupCakes, Rollovers, Great Danish, Bark'n'Fetch Biscuits, or Jump'n'Sit Bits? Dogs consider us the Ben & Jerry's of their world, and with good reason.

The fact is, we've been fresh-baking the world's best foods and treats for dogs since 1989—and our company's growth over the years is a *howling* success—testimony to the quality of the stuff we love to bake. We use only wholesome, healthy human-quality ingredients in all the tasty things we produce. We stay close to the earth in our ingredient selection to enable you, as a consumer, to know (and pronounce) what's in your dog's foods and treats—and to let you feel great about what you're serving. Plus, all-natural, high-quality ingredients will help your dog (who, after all, is the *real* consumer) live a happier and healthier life. It is a little-known fact that

99.9 percent of all dogs surveyed prefer whole grains, fruits, and vegetables to propylene glycol any day of the week. If dogs are ever "made" out of artificial material, maybe we'll feed them artificial "food product." But until then, our motto is: All-natural foods for your all-natural dog!

There has always been a profound love between dogs and their faithful human companions. However, what was expressed quietly in years past has now come screaming out of the doghouse and into the open. We've seen an *arf*ful lot of change in the wonderful world of dogs since those far-off days when folks went slack-jawed hearing that we had started a bakery for dogs. Today there are pet resorts, gyms,

bed and breakfasts, and canine nail salons—you might say that the world truly is going to the dogs.

It's easy to describe what your dog will discover inside a Three Dog Bakery: wholesome foods, tasty snacks, and fun toys. And ahhh . . . the aroma of Boxer Brownies wafting through the air! If you thought your dog loved you before, you'll be the Master of the Universe once s/he discovers that you know the directions to a Three Dog Bakery. And be sure to tell your dog that we're opening even more locations—we're coming soon to a neighborhood near you! But in the meantime, you can always click on over to our virtual bakery (www.threedog.com) for some *actual* treats.

How Did We Start the World's Most Unusual Bakery?

We started Three Dog Bakery practically by accident. If you read our last book, *Amazing Gracie,* you will know that Gracie, our precious, adorable, lovely (and no, we're not biased) deaf Great Dane pup (and, along with Dottie and Sarah Jean, the Biscuit Queen, one of our three canine cofounders), had stopped eating. Nothing we, or our vet, did would convince her to do otherwise. She seemed to be the world's only living anorexic dog—quite possibly in the entire history of the canine race. She got skinnier and skinnier, eventually

 **Finally—a *Good* Habit!**

Get in the daily habit of always measuring out your dog's food instead of just pouring it into her bowl. Overfeeding by merely 5 or 10 percent per day will add unhealthy pounds to your dog's frame. By keeping food amounts consistent, you can better control your dog's weight, and it will help reduce the urge to add "just a little more."

It's No Fun Being a Round Hound

Not surprisingly, as our nation's waistline expands, so do our dogs'. Obesity is now the number-1 health risk for dogs, too. Extra weight puts increased stress on your dog's skeletal system and can dramatically decrease your dog's expected life span. In Western countries, some research suggests, up to 40 percent of companion dogs are overweight. Carrying extra weight:

o Puts incredible stress on a dog's skeletal system and joints

o Aggravates arthritis and causes skin disease

o Affects a dog's immune system and ability to ward off disease and to heal after surgery

o Dramatically decreases your dog's expected life span

So please keep your dog at his proper "biting" weight!

looking gaunt and unhealthy. Finally, after all our desperate attempts to get Gracie to eat again, in desperation we (who could barely feed ourselves) began to cook for her. And suddenly, our beautiful baby started eating again. And eating. And eating.

Working with our vet, we began to educate ourselves about dog food and the different ingredients used in its production. We couldn't understand why a simple box of dog biscuits would sometimes contain over 50 ingredients—40 of which you couldn't pronounce, let alone understand why they were used. How could we look Sarah, Dottie, and Gracie in the eyes and tell them that the food they were eating had a longer shelf life than they did?

Why Did We Write This Cookbook?

People know us for our bakeries, our books, and our TV appearances, but we know that we owe most of our success to our wholesome and tasty recipes—a dreamy, drooly collection of healthful, gourmutt concoctions, designed especially for dogs. Over the years, we've developed thousands of recipes in our Three Dog Bakery kitchens. We focus on simplicity—easy-to-rustle-up (even easier to eat!) creations that

Introdogtion

As you and your dogs sniff through these recipes—cooking your way to hound dog heaven—we hope you will *paws* from time to time to enjoy and learn from the trivia, tips, factoids, and advice dispensed in these pages. Although they are presented in no particular order, they are all important. Well, mostly—and if they aren't actually important, we hope they'll at least be interesting and entertaining!

All of the ingredients used in this book are dog-friendly and can be used in the supplemental feeding of your dog—perfect for special occasions, celebrations, meals to bond over, or times when you must "encourage" an appetite in your pet. The recipes are not intended to be 100 percent complete diets for your dogs. If in doubt about any ingredient with respect to your own dogs, consult with your veterinarian. Naturally, you'll want always to opt for the freshest, healthiest foods available.

Here are some basic starting-out tips that apply to all the recipes. Some (or all) of them may seem obvious to you, but remember—common sense is only common once you know it!

o Cooking for your dog can be a great way to avoid wasting leftovers, but use fresh ingredients in all the recipes, never old, moldy foods or anything in the least bit suspicious.

o The ingredients lists are a starting point, not law, so use what you have on hand—but be sure to refer to the list of "forbidden" ingredients (onions, raisins, chocolate, etc., found on pages 12 and 13)

o Make sure dishes have cooled sufficiently before serving.

o Keep leftovers tightly wrapped and refrigerated.

o Feed portions sized appropriately to your dog and his or her own eating habits.

o Discard uneaten portions from the fridge after three days, unless you're absolutely sure it's OK (i.e., would *you* eat it?).

o Finally, make enough to insure your dog gets some!

dogs love and their humans understand, using ingredients that you can readily find in your own kitchen cabinets. Hey, we *know* it's hard enough to cook for yourself, so we try to make it as easy as possible to cook for your dog!

For the last 15 years, our company has been committed to changing the way we feed our dogs. It's a cause we embrace because we revel in the love we feel for our dogs, and we *know* our dogs make us better people. Through good food, we nourish the bonds that connect us to them. Good, healthful nutrition helps make good, healthy dogs. *We love dogs—and dogs love us!*

A lot of dog lovers laugh the first time they hear about what we do. We can't count how many times we've heard "My dog's not a picky eater!" or "My dog will eat just about anything!" And their dogs aren't unique—as a species, dogs are omnivores, which means there's very little

that they won't at least *try* to eat! (And sometimes, we think you'll agree, things can get pretty disgusting. We'll pause for a moment while you shudder at the memory of your own particularly revolting dog-will-eat-anything incident.)

So, as we were saying. . . . Dogs are also *opportunistic* eaters, which means they'll generally eat whatever is available at the moment. That's why it's so important that we, as their trusted servants, give them the food that will make them healthiest and happiest. And *that's* why we've put together this collection of our own favorite new recipes, true-to-life illustrations, tried-and-true tips, and guaranteed useless trivia. We want these easy, healthful recipes to show you a very different way to nourish your dog's tummy, your conscience, *and* your pocketbook.

Three Dog Bakery Is Not About Dog Food— We're About Food for Dogs!

Folks sometimes ask us why our recipes have so many "people ingredients." Our most basic principle is that we won't feed our dogs *anything* we wouldn't eat ourselves. That's why everything we make—and every recipe we create for you to make at home—uses only fresh, all-natural human-quality ingredients.

Unfortunately, the vast majority of companies producing "dog food" don't feel the way we do. Most commercial brands of dog food are made from low-end ingredients crammed with chemicals and preservatives, then sprayed with animal fat at the end of an extrusion process to fool the dog (and its human) into

 Ahhh . . . It Hits the "Spot"

Always keep fresh, clean water on hand for your dogs, 365 days a year, 24 hours a day.

thinking the "food" is actually palatable. Feed-grade ingredients are used because they are cheap. They are cheap because they are nearly devoid of anything nutritionally substantive. Typically, pet food ingredients come from the lowest end of the low end of the food scale. As far as we're concerned, that's exactly the wrong place to find them.

The pet food business has historically been a dirty industry. Some of the top names in pet food have been cited for deviant business practices. You never have to wait long before yet another shocking revelation in the pet food industry comes to light—everything from deceptive labeling practices to highly questionable protein sources. Toxic animals too sick or too loaded with antibiotics to be sold as food for humans are regularly ground up and used in dog feed. Flour and grains too dirty or too low in quality for human consumption are what makes the grade for dog feed. But there's always the "high end" stuff, right?

Wrong. Even many so-called premium dog foods contain large amounts of fillers, which basically help push the "food" through the dog. Many are made from disgusting protein sources, dirty feed-grade grains, preservatives, chemicals, and non-FDA-inspected minerals and vitamins. The higher price often pays for prettier packaging and expensive ad campaigns, when it doesn't just enrich the company that makes it.

Would you feed something like that to your family?

The good news, thanks to Three Dog Bakery and other small, caring companies nudging the entire market forward, is that over the past decade, there have been some major (and amazing) shifts in the way we feed our companion animals. We are starting to realize that, just like us, our pets truly are what they eat. The healthier and cleaner we eat, the better we look and feel. The same holds true for the dogs we love and cherish as true family members.

With Dogs All Things Are Possible

It has been our great pleasure to shake paws and commune a little with dogs all over the planet. We have met hundreds of thousands, maybe even millions, of dogs over the last 15 years. During our travels around the world, we've come truly to realize that dogs really aren't different from one another. Just like humans, all they want is love, food, shelter, and peace.

For example, when we visit our Three Dog Bakery shops in Japan, other than an obvious *human* language barrier, we might as well be in Des Moines when it comes to the dogs. Dogs speak the universal language of love. Dachs-

hunds and Chihuahuas in Tokyo love a tummy rub and a biscuit every bit as much as dogs do here in the United States.

With dogs by our sides, we're all the same. Dogs don't care if we're rich or poor, black or white, live in a mansion or a cardboard box. Dogs are the great equalizers, the great levelers. We're reminded of a quote from Roger Caras, author and past president of the ASPCA, who once said, "We give dogs the love we can spare, the time we can spare. In return dogs give us their absolute all. It is without a doubt the best deal man has ever made." Truer words were never spoken. We're all equal in a dog's eyes. (Well, except for that haughty French poodle down the street who looks down her pampered nose at us.)

Dogs unwittingly inspire us. They show us, by example, how to be better people. They live totally in the moment, 100 percent in the "now." No worrying about yesterday and what could have been. No chewing their paws, fretting about the future and if they'll have enough five years from now. They just live— here and now. Traveling light through life—a collar, a leash, a couple of bowls—dogs exemplify the simple life.

Dogs' innate ability to love us—to love us unconditionally, even when we don't deserve it—is their most wonderful trait. Theirs is a

 ## Doggie First Aid Kit

May you never need it, but keeping a well-stocked first aid kit is an *arf*fully good idea. You can get almost everything on this list at your local pharmacy. Ask your vet what else he or she would recommend. A basic kit would include, at minimum, these items:

- o Rolls of gauze (2 inch)
- o Adhesive tape
- o Latex gloves
- o Sterile pads
- o Small scissors and/or grooming clippers
- o Needle-nose pliers
- o Antibiotic cream (over the counter)

- o Rectal thermometer and petroleum jelly
- o Rubbing alcohol
- o Hydrogen peroxide
- o Nylon slip leash
- o Flashlight
- o Towels and a blanket

A stethoscope and a white smock with "Dr. Doggy" stitched over the pocket are optional.

higher form of love, which seems at times beyond our own ability to achieve. Love comes naturally to dogs, as if they're genetically wired for it. We've often wondered if it's mere coincidence that "dog" is "God" spelled backward. We can only imagine how beautiful the world could be if we were all a bit more like our dogs. To quote Roger Caras once more, "Dogs are not our whole life, but they make our life whole."

Warm Pawshakes to You and Your Dogs

As the years roll on, we are busier than ever cooking and baking for your dogs—and ours, too, of course. We would never have thought it was possible, but we love dogs more than ever. Nothing makes us happier than watching dogs romp alongside their humans—and knowing,

really *knowing,* that the world is a better place because of the bond between them. We hope that this book—its recipes, its tips, its trivia, its drawings, and its love—helps you strengthen the bond between you and the dog(s) in your life.

Yours drooly,

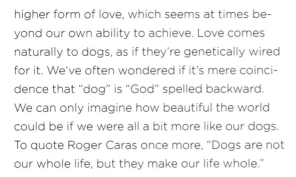

Dan Dye and Mark Beckloff, founders, Three Dog Bakery

Introdogtion

Our Pantry—and Yours!

Three Dog Bakery loves to stay close to the earth in the ingredients we select and use in all our recipes. Our treats and foods are prepared using whole grains, fruits, vegetables, herbs, and lean meats, such as USDA-inspected chicken. In fact, you'll be able to sniff out most of the ingredients used in this book in your own kitchen cabinets. This list will serve as a useful guide in helping you prepare your shopping list:

Grains
- All-purpose flour
- Whole wheat flour
- Barley
- Quick rolled oats
- Rice (extra long grain)

Fruits
- Apples
- Applesauce (no sugar added)
- Bananas
- Blueberries

Vegetables
- Carrots
- Frozen mixed vegetables
- Green beans
- Peas
- Potatoes
- Spinach

Herbs/Spices
- Cinnamon
- Garlic
- Oregano
- Parsley
- Rosemary
- Pure vanilla extract

Meat
- Chicken—skinless, boneless, USDA-inspected
- Chicken broth—canned, low-sodium (or save money and make your own!)
- Turkey, ground

Dairy
- Cream cheese, fat-free
- Eggs
- Parmesan cheese

- Skim milk
- Sour cream, low-fat
- Yogurt, plain, low-fat

Miscellaneous
- Baking powder
- Baking soda
- Bread crumbs
- Canola oil
- Carob chips—available at most health food stores
- Carob powder—available at most health food stores
- Cornstarch
- Honey
- Peanuts, unsalted
- Unsalted, all-natural peanut butter (unsweetened)

Golden Rule: If It's Bad for Us, It's Bad for Them!

Don't feed your dogs greasy, high-fat foods. They may love a fried treat just as we do, but it does them no more good than it does us, and it can be dangerous for them. High-fat foods and a sedentary lifestyle can lead your dog to obesity and pancreatitis. The pancreas produces enzymes that help people—and dogs—digest food. If dogs consume too much fat, the tissues around the pancreas break down and allow the digestive enzymes to leak out. It's a very common and painful ailment for dogs. Bouts of pancreatitis strike dogs most often around the holiday feasts. *Don't* feed your dogs turkey skin or other very fatty foods. Pancreatitis can put them into shock and, in some cases, can even be fatal.

Signs of Poisoning

Signs of poisoning include vomiting and/or diarrhea, seizures, trembling, salivating or drooling, swollen red skin or eyes, bleeding from any body cavity, ulcers on the skin, listlessness, and depression. Consult your vet at once if you have any reason to suspect that your pooch has been in contact with poison.

Forbidden Foods for Your Furry Friend

- **Alcoholic beverages** Can cause intoxication, coma, death.
- **Bones from fish, poultry, or other meat sources** Can cause obstruction or laceration of the digestive system.
- **Cat food** Generally too high in proteins and fats. Plus it has pictures of cats on it.
- **Chocolate and coffee** Contain theobromine and caffeine, which can be toxic and affect the heart, perhaps fatally.
- **Fat trimmings** Can cause pancreatitis.
- **Hops** Unknown compound causes increased heart rate, seizures, and death.
- **Human vitamin supplements containing iron** Can damage the lining of the digestive system and be toxic to the other organs, including the liver and kidneys.
- **Liver** In large amounts can cause vitamin A toxicity that affects muscles and bones.

- **Macadamia nuts** Contain an unknown toxin that can affect the digestive and nervous systems and muscles.

- **Marijuana** Can depress the nervous system and cause vomiting and changes in heart rate.

- **Moldy or spoiled food, garbage** Can contain any number of toxins that cause vomiting and diarrhea and also affect other organs.

- **Mushrooms** Wild-growing mushrooms—even the backyard variety—can contain toxins, which may affect multiple systems in the body, cause shock, and result in death.

- **Onions** Contains sulfoxides and disulfides, which can damage red blood cells and cause anemia.

- **Peach and plum pits** Can obstruct the digestive tract.

- **Persimmon seeds** Can cause intestinal obstruction and enteritis.

- **Raisins** Newly discovered to contain unknown toxins that may damage the kidneys when consumed in quantity.

- **Raw eggs** Contain an enzyme called avidin, which decreases the absorption of biotin, a B vitamin. This can lead to skin, hair, and coat problems. Raw eggs also may contain salmonella.

- **Raw fish** Can result in a thiamine (B vitamin) deficiency leading to loss of appetite, seizures, and sometimes death. The problem is more common if raw fish is fed regularly.

- **Salt** Large quantities may lead to electrolyte imbalances.

- **String** Can become trapped in the digestive system and entwine around internal organs.

- **Sugary foods** Can lead to obesity, dental problems, and diabetes.

- **Table scraps** Should never make up more than 10 percent of the diet, if that.

- **Tobacco** Contains nicotine, which damages the nervous and digestive systems. Can result in rapid heartbeat, collapse, coma, and death. Not to mention how ridiculous dogs look trying to hold the cigarette.

- **Yeast dough** Can expand and produce gas in the digestive system, causing pain and possible rupture of the stomach and intestines.

Source: The National Animal Poison Control Center

Our Pantry—and Yours!

Yappetizers

A dog can express more with his tail
in minutes than his owner can express
with his tongue in hours.

—Unknown

*T*here must be a thousand and one reasons to whip up a tray of *yap*-petizers, the little snacks intended to whet the appetite (as if our dogs need more motivation for *that* to happen!). Any time dogs are gathered together is a doggone good opportunity to have a few snacks around, or even when your dog is home alone with you and you just want a change of pace from your usual treat. Some occasions just cry out for a special snack: first visit to the vet's office, obedience school graduation, welcome home from the kennel (what better way to apologize?), the birthday party for the dog next door, congratulations on the nine new puppies—when you think of it, what occasion *isn't* a good excuse for a fresh-baked snack?

The following *yap*petizer recipes are meant to *arf*fer inspiration for those occasions when love—and fur—is in the air.

Mad Dogs and Englishmen Savory Scones

The ideal snack for British breeds and dogs
who like to hightail it to high tea.

○ Makes 12 *hair*istocratic scones ○

There's nothing like high tea at London's famous Battersea Dogs' Home—the *pup* and circumstance, the plummy accents ("I say, old boy, fetch me one of those rawhide sticks, would you? There's a good chap. . . .")—and the mad-dog rush for the savory scones that makes American football look like a . . . well, like a tea party!

1 cup all-purpose flour
2 teaspoons baking powder
¼ cup olive oil
1 cup grated light cheddar cheese
½ cup diced cooked chicken
½ cup plus 2 tablespoons skim milk

Preheat the oven to 400°F. Grease a baking sheet with nonstick vegetable spray.

Stir together the flour and baking powder in a large bowl. Pour the olive oil into the flour mixture and stir until thoroughly blended. Stir in the cheese and chicken. Add ½ cup milk to make a soft dough.

. . . With Two to Four Inches of Cats Expected in the Suburbs

The term "raining cats and dogs" can be traced to medieval times in England. During heavy rains and the flooding that followed, bodies of cats and dogs could be seen floating through the gutters and narrow streets, creating the illusion that it had "rained cats and dogs."

Turn the dough out onto a lightly floured surface and knead gently until smooth. With a rolling pin, roll the dough out to ¾-inch thickness. Cut into 2-inch rounds with a cookie cutter or glass and place on the baking sheet. Brush each biscuit with the remaining milk and bake for 17 to 20 minutes, or until the cheese bits begin to bubble and lightly brown.

Cool to room temperature before serving.

Store in an airtight container for up to 5 days, or wrap well and freeze for up to 2 months. (Thaw before serving.)

 Teatime!

An infusion tea made from rosemary and lemon makes a soothing coat tonic and herbal conditioner. The rosemary produces a wonderful fragrance and promotes a shiny coat, and the lemon adds fragrance and helps repel parasites.

o **Bring to a boil 1 quart water. Remove from heat and add 2 teaspoons dried rosemary and ½ lemon. Cover and steep for 10 to 15 minutes.**

o **Let the tea cool completely to room temperature, then strain.**

o **After your dog's bath, pour the tea gently over her entire coat.**

o **Towel dry.**

Zippity Zucchini Terrier Tortes

Dogs love vegetables—they'd eat healthy
if we'd help them do it!

○ Makes 12 *terrier*ific tortes ○

After catching a few *z*'s yourself, these are the perfect way to add some zest and flavor to your dog's afternoon. Fresh shredded zucchini provides natural moistness and texture to these simple cakes—a de*tail* that's sure to be sniffed out by your little zipper!

 You Make Me Feel *Bran* New

A light sprinkling of wheat bran on your dog's regular daily food will help to increase her fiber intake as she ages.

2 cups whole wheat flour
1 tablespoon baking powder
1 teaspoon ground cinnamon
¼ cup canola oil
¼ cup honey
1 cup skim milk
2 large eggs
1 cup shredded zucchini

Preheat the oven to 375°F. Grease a 12-cup muffin pan with nonstick vegetable spray.

Stir together the flour, baking powder, and cinnamon in a large bowl and set aside. In a separate bowl, whisk together the oil, honey, milk, and ½ cup water until smooth. Add the eggs, one at a time, and then the zucchini. Add the wet ingredients to the dry ingredients and stir just until moistened.

Fill the muffin cups ⅔ full. Bake for 20 to 25 minutes, or until a toothpick inserted in the center of a muffin comes out clean.

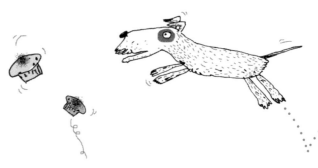

Cool to room temperature before serving.

Store in an airtight container for up to 3 days, or wrap well and freeze for up to 2 months. (Thaw before serving.)

Fiber and Fido

Fiber plays an important role in your dog's diet. Fiber absorbs water and helps move things along in the intestines. However, make sure your dog's food doesn't contain more fiber than necessary. Ask your vet the optimal amount of fiber your dog's diet should contain. Some common sources of fiber found in many commercial dog foods include beet pulp, rice bran, peanut hulls, and cellulose.

Mighty Mites

If your dog shakes her head, paws at her ears, rubs the side of her face against furniture or carpeting, but doesn't show signs of infection (inflamed, swollen, tender, oozing) in her ears, it may be mites. Look for dark debris or grit inside ears. Keep her ears clean and dry to help prevent mites from burrowing into her ears.

Yappetizers

Say "Cheese!" Tail Chasers

Yum—these taste so *gouda*! An "it's-all-about-me" treat for dogs who like to strut their stuff for the *pup*arazzi—or the cat next door.

○ **Makes 12 tail chasers** ○

Gossip columnists in the world of canine celebrities constantly *hound* us for tempting tidbits or mouthwatering morsels. These muffins are often just the dish they're looking for.

 Open Wide

Did you know that to get a serious visit-to-the-dentist's-office kind of teeth cleaning, a dog must be anesthetized *completely*?

1 cup all-purpose flour
1 cup whole wheat flour
1 tablespoon baking powder
1 large egg
½ cup skim milk
2 tablespoons canola oil
1 tablespoon honey
½ cup grated light cheddar cheese

Preheat the oven to 400°F. Grease a 12-cup muffin pan with nonstick vegetable spray.

Stir together the flours and baking powder in a large bowl and set aside. In a separate bowl, whisk together the egg, milk, oil, and honey with 1 cup of water until smooth. Add the wet ingredients to the dry ingredients and stir just until combined. Gently fold in the cheese.

Fill the muffin cups ⅔ full. Bake for 20 minutes, or until a toothpick inserted in the center of a muffin comes out clean.

Cool to room temperature before serving.

Store in an airtight container for up to 3 days, or wrap well and freeze for up to 2 months. (Thaw before serving.)

It's Crunch Time

If your dog's teeth continue to be in good shape, keep feeding dry, crunchy kibble. It helps teeth, gums, and mouth tissue to stay healthy, reduces tartar buildup, and helps prevent tooth decay and gum disease.

Are You Smilin' at Me?!

It can be hard not to smile when you see a pooch, but grinning at a dog you don't know can be hazardous to your health. Dogs can interpret baring your teeth as a sign of aggression toward them and respond accordingly. Same thing goes for staring directly into a dog's eyes.

SAY CHEESE

Clickity Click.

La Biscuit Exquisite

Elegant simplicity baked into a biscuit.

○ **Makes 12 servings, worthy of top hats and *tails*** ○

From pampered pooches on Fifth Avenue to mangy mutts on Main Street, it's always the simple things in life that are the doggone best. This is a timeless yet simple treat to pique the palate of your precious, pampered pooch.

If You Can't Pronounce It, They Shouldn't Eat It

Inspect your dog's food label carefully. Avoid any foods and treats that contain artificial preservatives, chemicals, and coloring agents.

And if you *can* pronounce it but you don't know what it is . . . better safe than sorry.

2 cups all-purpose flour
2 teaspoons baking powder
2 tablespoons molasses
2 tablespoons canola oil
1 cup buttermilk

Preheat the oven to 375°F. Grease a baking sheet with nonstick vegetable spray.

Stir together the flour and baking powder in a large bowl. Stir in the molasses and oil until the mixture is blended. Slowly stir in the buttermilk to form a soft dough.

On a lightly floured surface, roll the dough out with a rolling pin to ¼-inch thickness. Cut into 2-inch rounds with a cookie cutter or glass and place on the baking sheet.

Bake the biscuits for 15 minutes, or until light golden in color.

Cool to room temperature before serving.

Store in an airtight container for up to 1 week, or wrap well and freeze for up to 2 months. (Thaw before serving.)

 Read Before You Feed!

Read the ingredient panel on your dog's food and be aware of labeling loopholes. Avoid foods containing the chemical ethoxyquin, which is a toxic substance used to preserve fats (and rubber!). Call dog food manufacturers to make *sure* that ethoxyquin is not present—they're not legally required to list it if it's already been added to the fat they're buying.

 Shocking!

Puppies love to chew; for some reason, they especially seem to enjoy electrical cords. It's important to take the time to identify any and all electrical cords and place them out of temptation's way whenever possible. If your pup begins to play with an electrical cord, spray it with bitter apple spray (available at any pet store) or rub it with hot chili paste to discourage further interest. Chili paste is hot, but not as hot as a 1,200-volt charge.

Twice-as-Nice-per-Slice Spice Bread

Add a little spice to your dog's life.

○ **Makes 6 spice-and-everything-nice loaves** ○

There's something about the smart snap of ginger, sweetened with cinnamon, honey, and molasses, that always makes our dogs come running. And once they've wolfed—or dogged—it down, well . . . can it be only *our* dogs who prance around with a little extra zing? Try it on your best friends and let us know.

½ cup canola oil
½ cup honey
1 large egg
½ cup molasses
2½ cups all-purpose flour
2 teaspoons ground ginger
2 teaspoons ground cinnamon
1 teaspoon baking powder

Preheat the oven to 350°F. Grease 6 disposable aluminum mini-loaf pans with nonstick vegetable spray.

Whisk together the oil and honey in a large bowl. Beat in the egg and molasses until the mixture is smooth. In a separate bowl, combine the flour, ginger, cinnamon, and baking powder, and add to the molasses mixture. Pour ½ cup hot tap water over the batter and stir gently.

Fill the mini-loaf pans ⅔ full. Bake for 35 to 40 minutes, or until a toothpick inserted in the center of a loaf comes out clean.

Cool to room temperature before serving.

Store in an airtight container for up to 3 days, or wrap well and freeze for up to 2 months. (Thaw before serving.)

Dark Dangers of the Doggy Domain

You come home. You look around. Same ol' place—lots of things you might change if you could, but, hey, it's home, right? Wrong—your seemingly warm and welcoming abode is a potential *canine catastrophe!* Everywhere you turn are outwardly benign items that could turn terrible without a moment's notice. In other words, we're talking about pretty much anything our dogs *can* get in their mouths but *shouldn't!*

Some of the most common household dangers are:

o Antifreeze

o Caffeine

o Chocolate

o Drugs—prescription *and* over the counter!

o Electrical cords

o Fertilizers

o Herbicides

o Household cleaning agents

o Insecticides

o Paint

o Rodent poisons and traps

o Swimming pool cleaners

It's not that we can't have these things, of course, but please store them in places where your dog can't get to them. And when you're using them, be very aware of the dog's potential access!

Yappetizers

Little Eataly Meatballs

Move over, s*paw*ghetti—it's time to chow down!

o **Makes 24 *mutt* balls** o

Despite everything we've done to help them cultivate highly sophisticated palates, our dogs would happily eat ground meat straight from the package—even frozen—as a matter of fact, at least one we could name would consider the package a tasty garnish. But that doesn't mean they don't *appreciate* our doing something more to the meat than bringing it home! Plus, it never hurts that the oats are a great source of fiber, vitamins B_1, B_2, and E, and the eggs give them those nice, silky coats.

Brusha, Brusha, Brusha

Brushing your dog's teeth every day will prevent tartar buildup, tooth decay, and gum disease, which lead to greater problems like heart disease. Give your dog's teeth a short brushing every day—even if it's just the front teeth and fangs—and you'll help him stay healthier longer. Besides, it's a lot easier than teaching him to gargle and floss.

2 cups quick rolled oats
2 large eggs
2 pounds ground chicken or turkey
½ cup grated Parmesan cheese
1 teaspoon dried oregano
½ teaspoon garlic powder

Preheat the oven to 350°F.

Combine all the ingredients in a large bowl and mix well, using your hands. Scoop out a tablespoon or two of the mixture and roll it

into a ball. Continue with the rest of the mixture.

Place the meatballs on an ungreased shallow baking pan. Bake for 40 minutes.

Cool to room temperature before serving.

Store in a covered container in the refrigerator for up to 3 days, or wrap well and freeze for up to 2 months. (Thaw before serving.)

 ## No Raw Eggs or Meat!

Don't feed raw eggs to your dog. Raw eggs contain an enzyme called avidin, which inhibits the absorption of biotin, a B vitamin that plays an important role in maintaining healthy skin and coat. Raw eggs may contain salmonella, a nasty bacteria that causes nausea, fever, intestinal cramping, and explosive diarrhea.

 ## A Close Brush

Daily brushing will help keep your dog's coat shiny and healthy, but it also gives you an opportunity to inspect your dog for lumps, bumps, fleas, ticks, hot spots, scrapes, or any other maladies. It also gives you a great excuse to spend quality one-on-one time with your dog. Always brush your dog before giving her a bath, or else mats and clumps in the fur will be impossible to comb out. If a knot is bad when the fur is dry, it'll be worse wet!

Peanut Brindle

A totally tasty, tail-wagging treat—
a terrific twist on an all-American classic!

○ **Makes 25 naturally nutty servings** ○

Not your grandma's teeth-cracking version of peanut brittle, it's the up-to-date canine confection for the new millennium. Rice flour lends a slightly sweet, faintly nutty flavor (and we mean that with all due respect). A fresh-baked tray wrapped in a pretty box or gift tin is a great way to say "Welcome to the neighborhood" to a new neighbor pup.

3½ cups rice flour
1 teaspoon ground cinnamon
½ teaspoon baking powder
1 egg
¼ cup honey
¼ cup unsalted peanut butter
½ cup canola oil
1 teaspoon pure vanilla extract
½ cup chopped unsalted peanuts

Preheat the oven to 325°F. Grease a jelly roll pan with nonstick vegetable spray.

Stir together the rice flour, cinnamon, and baking powder in a bowl and set aside. In a large bowl, whisk together the egg, honey, peanut butter, oil, and vanilla. Add the dry ingredients to the wet ingredients, and add 1 cup water. Stir to form a stiff batter.

Turn the dough out onto the jelly roll pan. Cover the dough with plastic wrap. With a rolling pin, roll the dough out evenly to ¼-inch thickness. Remove the plastic wrap and sprin-

kle the dough with peanuts, lightly pressing them into the dough. Score the dough with a knife into 2 X 3-inch rectangles.

Bake for 30 to 40 minutes, or until the edges begin to turn golden brown.

Cool to room temperature in the pan before breaking apart along the score lines and serving.

Store in an airtight container for up to 1 week, or wrap well and freeze for up to 2 months. (Thaw before serving.)

CRUNCH
CRUNCH

Beware the Perilous Plant!

Sure, they may *look* harmless enough, but to dogs they can be poisonous—anywhere from dangerous to deadly. The problem is bored dogs with nothing but time on their paws *love* to chew houseplants and garden plants. Dogs love to dig in freshly tilled soil, so bulbs are especially tempting. Be extra careful of:

o **Buttercups**

o **Caladium**

o **Calla lily**

o **Crocus bulbs**

o **Daffodil bulbs**

o **Easter lily bulbs**

o **Hemlock**

o **Hydrangea**

o **Jonquil bulbs**

o **Lily of the valley**

o **Mistletoe**

o **Narcissus bulbs**

o **Oleander**

o **Poinsettia**

o **Skunk cabbage (not to mention skunks!)**

o **Yew**

Yappetizers

Pupeye's Grrrrrreek Spanielkopita

If Olive Oyl had made these, things might have worked out differently with Popeye.

○ Makes 16 *mutt*iterranean servings ○

Remember, dogs—even Popeye's dog Jeep—don't know that spinach is a vegetable and they're supposed to hate it. Dogs actually like spinach, and it's full of nutrients and iron, including St. Bernard–size helpings of healthy vitamins.

1 cup all-purpose flour
1 teaspoon baking powder
2 large eggs, beaten
¼ cup olive oil
1 cup skim milk
1 cup grated low-fat cheddar cheese
One 10-ounce package frozen chopped spinach,
    thawed and drained

Preheat the oven to 350°F. Grease an 8 X 8-inch square pan with nonstick vegetable spray.

Stir together the flour and baking powder in a large bowl and set aside. In a separate bowl, whisk together the eggs, olive oil, and milk. Add the wet ingredients to the dry ingredients and stir until smooth. Stir in the cheese and spinach.

Spread the batter evenly in the pan. Bake for 35 minutes, or until light golden.

Cut into squares. Cool completely before serving.

Store in the refrigerator for up to 3 days, or wrap tightly and freeze for up to 2 months. (Thaw before serving.)

My, How Many Teeth You Have

A dog has 42 teeth—10 more than we do (if we have them all).

Pupovers

A snack for dogs looking to take the edge off the hunger
that hits them between meals—or between snacks.

○ **Makes 12 habit-forming servings** ○

The news will be barked over backyard fences about this treat, so don't be surprised if the neighborhood dogs pop over for *pup*overs!

6 large egg whites
1 cup skim milk
2 tablespoons canola oil
1 cup all-purpose flour
Honey

Preheat the oven to 375°F. Grease a 12-cup muffin pan with nonstick vegetable spray.

In a large bowl, beat the egg whites with an electric mixer until soft peaks form. In a small bowl, whisk together the milk and oil until blended. Gently stir the milk/oil mixture into the egg whites. Fold in the flour until the batter is smooth.

Fill the muffin cups ⅔ full. Bake for 30 minutes, or until light golden.

Cool to room temperature. Drizzle lightly with honey and serve.

Store in an airtight container for up to 3 days, or wrap well and freeze for up to 2 months. (Thaw before serving.)

SALIVATIN' SUGGESTION: Fully cooked lean meat may be added. To do so, simply fill the muffin cups ⅓ full with batter, add a spoonful of chopped meat, then cover meat with more batter. Bake as directed. Store in an airtight container in the refrigerator.

Garçon, Cancel the Steak Tartare

Feeding your dog raw meat increases his chance of contracting parasites and dangerous bacteria like salmonella.

Pawtite Pies

You don't need to be a miniature breed
to enjoy these bite-size tarts.

○ Makes 12 paw-lickin' *paw*stries ○

No *paw*ty is complete without *Paw*tite Pies. Put on a Three Dog Night CD, and watch your party hounds get down. Even if your dogs are *paw*ticular, we're *paw*sitive they'll *paw*litely ask for more!

 He's All Ears

According to the *Guinness Book of World Records,* a basset hound in the United Kingdom named Mr. Jeffries has the longest ears in the world. They measure almost a foot long each!

Don't even bother whispering—he can probably hear what you're *thinking!*

DOUGH
½ cup canola oil
One 3-ounce package fat-free cream cheese, softened
1 cup all-purpose flour

Grease a 12-cup mini-muffin pan with nonstick vegetable spray.

Beat together the oil and cream cheese in a bowl until smooth. Mix in the flour to form a soft dough.

Divide the dough into 12 pieces and press into the mini-muffin cups.

 Bathtime Tips

Only use high-quality doggie shampoos when bathing your dog. Human shampoos are formulated to a different pH balance and can dry your dog's skin or cause a rash or irritation.

FILLING
1 large egg, beaten
½ cup honey
1 tablespoon canola oil
½ tablespoon pure vanilla extract

Preheat the oven to 400°F.

Combine all the filling ingredients in a bowl and mix until smooth. Divide the filling among the pastry-lined muffin cups.

Bake for 15 minutes, or until the shells are light golden.

Cool to room temperature before serving.

Store in an airtight container in the refrigerator for up to 3 days, or wrap well and freeze for up to 2 months. (Thaw before serving.)

You Dirty Dog!

Bathe your dog as needed, but don't worry about keeping him overly clean. Give him a bath when he feels and smells dirty, greasy, or itchy. Inserting cotton balls in your dog's ears right before his bath will help prevent water getting into the ears—which dogs hate. Placing a nonskid mat on the bottom of your tub will help your dog feel more secure. It's a good idea to make bathwater a few degrees cooler than you might think comfortable. Never give your dog the kind of "hot, relaxing" bath you'd like for yourself. Normally a bath once a month is a good rule of thumb, er, paw. (Once every five years, if you ask your dog.) Wear old, comfy clothes—or nothing at all!—to give your dog a bath. You will get wet.

Yappetizers

(Baying at the) Harvest Moon Apple Cake

Winner "Best Singing Inspiration" at the annual
Hounds-of-the-Baskervilles Bake-off

○ **Makes 12 to 15 howlingly good servings** ○

The first autumn nip is in the air, you're baying at the moon, and there's nothing better to give you those extra decibels than a nice big piece of Harvest Moon Apple Cake. Ah-OOOOOOoooooohhhhh!

2 cups all-purpose flour
1 teaspoon baking powder
2 large eggs, beaten
½ cup honey
½ cup canola oil
1 tablespoon pure vanilla extract
1 medium apple, cored and chopped

Preheat the oven to 350°F. Grease a 9 X 13-inch pan with nonstick vegetable spray.

Combine the flour and baking powder in a large bowl and set aside. In a separate bowl, whisk together the eggs, honey, oil, and vanilla until smooth. Add the wet ingredients to the dry ingredients and stir just until moistened. Fold in the apple.

Pour the batter into the greased pan and smooth the top.

Bake for 40 minutes, or until a toothpick inserted into the center of the cake comes out clean.

Cool completely before serving.

Store in an airtight container for 3 days, or wrap well and freeze for up to 2 months. (Thaw before serving.)

Fangs for the Memories

A puppy's teeth begin falling out at four to five months of age. The last of the adult teeth to come in are the "fangs," which are usually grown in by six months of age.

Biscotti Bites

Hey! Who needs ca*pooch*ino? These are great without dunking!

o Makes about 4 dozen biscotti—a favorite from Scotties to Rotties o

You don't have to be an Italian greyhound to appreciate these fresh and festive treats, baked twice for twice the flavor. The extra-crunchy texture helps clean canine choppers, too.

2½ cups all-purpose flour
2 teaspoons baking powder
3 tablespoons canola oil
6 tablespoons honey
2 large eggs
1 teaspoon pure vanilla extract
¼ cup chopped unsalted peanuts

Preheat the oven to 350°F. Grease a baking sheet with nonstick vegetable spray.

Stir together the flour and baking powder in a large bowl and set aside. In a separate bowl, whisk together the canola oil and honey until well blended. Add the eggs, one at a time, and then the vanilla, stirring to combine. Add the wet ingredients to the dry ingredients and stir to form a smooth dough. Mix in the peanuts.

Divide the dough in half and form each half into a log about 12 inches long and 4 inches wide.

Place the logs on the baking sheet. Bake 14 to 16 minutes, or until golden brown.

Transfer the logs to a cutting board, cool 5 minutes, and slice at a 45-degree angle, about ½ inch thick. Place the slices on the baking sheet and bake for an additional 10 to 12 minutes to dry slightly.

Transfer the biscotti to wire racks to cool. Cool completely before serving.

Store in an airtight container for up to 1 week, or wrap well and freeze for up to 2 months. (Thaw before serving.)

Yappetizers

Original Biscuits

And we do mean ORIGINAL. A teatime treat that will delight
English bulldogs, setters, and sheepdogs.

○ **Makes approximately 24 prim and proper Victorian biscuits, depending on size** ○

I'm Not Starving, I'm *Cleansing!*

A dog may fast naturally to improve health (something that's *never* happened in this household—since Gracie!). No need to force your dog to eat for a day or two, and there is *usually* no need to worry, if he is naturally refusing his food. A day or two of fasting (again, just like for us) does the body good. It allows the body's organs to grind up and break down accumulated toxins. You should not force a dog to eat or "dress" his food up to entice his appetite.

Someone gave us this recipe in a dark alley on a foggy night under a street-lamp and swore it was the world's original dog biscuit recipe, dating back at *least* to Victorian England. Before we could question him, he was gone. We pawed through our box of treasures to find it—and here it is, for your baking pleasures.

1½ cups all-purpose flour
¼ cup quick rolled oats
2 tablespoons baking powder
3 tablespoons canola oil
2 tablespoons honey
2 tablespoons skim milk (OK, skim milk is our modification)

Preheat the oven to 400°F. Grease a baking sheet with nonstick vegetable spray.

Stir together the flour, oats, and baking powder in a large bowl. Stir in the oil and honey until the mixture is well blended. Add the milk slowly to form a stiff dough.

Turn the dough out onto a lightly floured surface and knead gently until smooth. With a rolling pin, roll the dough out to ¼-inch thickness.

Use a fork to poke holes evenly across the surface of the dough. Cut the dough into desired shapes with cookie cutters or a glass. Place the biscuits on the baking sheet and bake for 10 minutes, or until golden brown.

Cool completely before serving.

Store in an airtight container for up to 1 week, or wrap well and freeze for up to 2 months. (Thaw before serving.)

 It's All about Balance

A dog requires balanced nutrition, just as we do. Don't overfeed meat to your dog, or she may develop health problems or system imbalances. A wild dog, left to her own wily devices, will eat a wide variety of plants, vegetables, and seeds, in addition to hunting down protein sources.

Yappetizers

Socializing your puppy is absolutely one of the most important things you can do for her. The age from 3 weeks to 20 weeks is critical in your dog's development. Many of the experiences your dog has at this stage and during these formative weeks will leave indelible imprints on her future, life-long behavior.

During this stage, it is crucial to introduce your pup to as many new and positive experiences as possible. By doing so, you will be helping your dog feel well adjusted and comfortable in almost any situation or setting. Allow her to be in situations where she can be handled, played with, handfed by a variety of people. After your pup has had all her shots, allow her to meet and play with as many new dogs as possible. This is an important step in puppy development, in which she will learn to be a dog and how to interact properly with her world. It is very important, during socialization, to make these "outside" experiences as positive and stress-free as possible.

The socialization process should continue throughout doggie adolescence and young adulthood, at a minimum. Exposing your puppy to many experiences and in as pleasurable a manner as possible will teach her that the world is a nice place and that people and other dogs are to be considered friends.

Shelters are full of dogs who were not properly socialized and, as adult dogs, became aggressive, untrusting, and uncontrollable. Socialization may not help 100 percent of the dogs 100 percent of the time, but in the vast majority of cases it's a major contribution toward a happy, healthy, well-adjusted dog down the road.

Garden of Eatin' Veggie Bread

Your dog will be only too happy to help you
dig up the garden for the ingredients.

○ Makes a *barker's* dozen of wholesome, healthy helpings ○

It's a vegetarian banquet baked into a little loaf of bread. Lots of fresh veggies and herbs add subtle hints of sweet and savory to the mix. There's just something so unabashedly wholesome and friendly about this recipe. See if your dog agrees. Ours do.

3 cups all-purpose flour
1 cup wheat germ
1 tablespoon baking powder
2 tablespoons olive oil
¼ cup molasses
1 large egg
½ cup grated carrot
½ cup grated zucchini
¼ cup chopped fresh parsley
¼ teaspoon dried rosemary

Preheat the oven to 350°F. Grease a 9 X 13-inch casserole dish with nonstick vegetable spray.

Stir together the flour, wheat germ, and baking powder in a large bowl and set aside. In a separate bowl, whisk together the olive oil and molasses. Add the egg and 1¼ cups water and mix to combine. Add the wet ingredients to the dry ingredients and mix until smooth. Fold in the carrots, zucchini, parsley, and rosemary.

Pour the batter into the casserole dish. Bake for 50 to 60 minutes, or until a toothpick inserted in the center comes out clean.

Cool completely before serving.

Store in an airtight container for up to 3 days, or wrap well and freeze for up to 2 months. (Thaw before serving.)

Yappetizers

DINNER WILL BE SERVED AT 6 O'CLOCK SHARP

Entrées

$\mathcal{C}$ooking for your dogs at home is one of the best things you can *paw*sibly do for them, or one of the worst—and not just because of your culinary skills! Dogs require balanced, complete nutrition to maintain optimal health and vigor throughout their lives. If you are absolutely sure you can provide that level of detail in your dog's diet, then there's nothing better you could do for him or her. If, however, you can't go to that length, or you're merely guessing at what your dog needs, you'd be courting dire doggie disaster—and you might end up doing your best friend more harm than good!

The following entrée recipes are provided not as a complete daily diet for your dog, but for those times when you might just want to provide some healthful extra nurturing—a little lovin' from your oven. And may they motivate you always to put high-quality, healthful dinners in your pup's supper bowl.

If you can't decide between a shepherd, a setter, or a poodle, get them all . . . adopt a mutt.

—ASPCA

Pawsta Salad

Inspired by all the Italian dogs we know—it's great for
energetic dogs who love to ciao down!

○ **Makes approximately 6 southern Italian "say-it-with-your-paws" servings** ○

Light, refreshing, and best of all, easy to make—just a great year-round dish. Pasta has been used to feed critters for centuries. Lots of carbs, proteins, and other nutrients—and extremely versatile, too. Use the pasta you have in your cupboard, and toss it with fresh vegetables, cheese, and/or cubed chicken for a nutritious, quick meal.

1 cup macaroni, shell, elbow, or bow-tie pasta
½ cup shredded mozzarella cheese
1 cup diced cooked chicken
½ cup diced carrots
½ cup diced green beans
1 tablespoon chopped fresh parsley
⅓ cup diced fresh tomatoes
Dressing (recipe follows)

Bring a large pot of water to a boil. Cook the pasta until al dente (firm to the tooth—or fang, as the case may be). Drain the pasta, place it in a large bowl, and toss with the cheese while still warm. Stir in the chicken, carrots, green beans, parsley, and tomatoes.

Pour the dressing over the pasta mixture and toss gently.

Cool to room temperature before serving.

Store covered in the refrigerator for up to 3 days.

Dressing

½ teaspoon dried basil
1 tablespoon canola oil
2 tablespoons buttermilk

In a small bowl, mix together the basil, oil, and buttermilk for the dressing.

Bloat Is Not Gas!

It happened to our big baby Gracie! Large dogs can be prone to a condition known as gastric torsion, or simply "bloat." Air or food fills the stomach and causes it to turn, cutting off the blood supply. The signs are restlessness and pacing, excessive drooling, swelling of the stomach area, and shock. Bloat often (but not always) occurs shortly after eating a big meal. Although there is no sure-fire prevention, experts recommend feeding your dog two smaller meals a day instead of one large one and *never* letting your dog "graze" and gorge from a bulk food source. Limit water intake at any one time, and don't let your dog get vigorous exercise less than an hour before or after eating.

Bloating is a mortally serious, life-threatening condition. Don't delay seeking immediate—and we mean IMMEDIATE—emergency attention! Even a few minutes can mean the difference between life and death for your dog.

Chicken Soup

Helps sick, ailing, and/or recovering dogs get back
into top bunny-chasing form.

○ **Makes a 2-day supply for an on-the-mend, medium-size dog** ○

Veterinarians frequently recommend cooking chicken soup for your pooch while he's recuperating. The soup provides a way to rehydrate an under-the-weather dog who might not be eating food or drinking water. Plus chicken soup is the miracle cure for all living beings, it seems. You *can* use canned chicken soup, but be sure to use low sodium or sodium free. But if you make it yourself you'll give your dog better food *and* save lots of money—and that'll make you feel better, too!

12 cups Homemade Chicken Stock (recipe
  follows) or canned, low-sodium chicken broth
1 cup long-grain rice
cooked and mashed carrots from Homemade
  Chicken Stock
2 cups cooked and shredded chicken

Bring the chicken stock to a boil in a large stockpot. Add the rice and carrots. Boil for 20 minutes, or until the rice is tender. Remove from the heat and add the chicken. Cool to room temperature before serving. Store covered in the refrigerator for up to 3 days.

It's Fun to Play Doctor, But . . .

Consult your vet before giving your dog *any* medicines. Some common over-the-counter medicines, such as Tylenol, can be toxic to your pet!

Homemade Chicken Stock

3½-pound whole chicken
2 to 3 carrots, peeled and trimmed
1 teaspoon ground thyme
1 teaspoon dried rosemary

Place the chicken in 4 quarts water in a large stockpot. Bring to a boil. Add the carrots, thyme, and rosemary. Gently simmer for 1 hour, skimming excess fat off the top, until the chicken is cooked through.

Remove the chicken from the stock. Carefully separate the chicken meat from the skin and bones, and set aside. Reserve the stock and discard the skin and bones. Remove the carrots, place them in a small bowl, mash them with a fork, and set aside.

 A Spoonful of Cream Cheese Helps the Medicine Go Down

Hiding a pill in a dab of fat-free cream cheese or peanut butter is a great way to "trick" your dog into swallowing a pill. Just make sure the pill goes down along with the treat. Some dogs are masters of spitting the pill out afterward when you're not looking!

Labrador Lasagna

Back by *pup*ular demand!
Here's a tail-waggin' twist on our original Labrador Lasagna.

○ **Makes 10 *molti buono* Labrador lunch roll-ups** ○

Mama mia! We love this recipe for lots of reasons—it's so easy and almost im-*paws*ible to ruin. *Paws*ta is an economical dish to prepare and has been served historically, and at times hysterically, to dogs throughout the world. Pasta, of course, is a good source of carbohydrates and vitamin A, and when you throw in fresh vegetables, as we do here, well, you've got a meal fit for a Medici (or would that be *Mutt*ici?).

1 cup low-fat cottage cheese

One 10-ounce package frozen chopped spinach, thawed and drained

10 lasagna noodles, cooked and drained

2 tablespoons all-purpose flour

1½ cups Homemade Chicken Stock (page 45) or canned, low-sodium chicken broth

¼ cup finely chopped or grated carrots

½ cup finely chopped or grated zucchini

½ teaspoon dried oregano

1 tablespoon finely chopped fresh parsley

Preheat the oven to 350°F. Grease a 9 X 13-inch baking pan with nonstick cooking spray.

Mix together the cottage cheese and spinach in a bowl. Spread 2 tablespoons of the mixture on each noodle and roll up. Place each roll, seam side down, in the baking pan and set aside.

In a saucepan, whisk together the flour and chicken broth until smooth. Cook over

Dog Cookies
Carroll Jans,
Special Sections

½ c. margarine
1 can beef broth or
2 c. bouillon
¼ c. brown sugar
1 t. garlic powder
1T. worcestershire sauce
1 egg
½ c. powdered milk
1 ½ c. oatmeal
1 ½ c. corn meal
3-4 c. whole wheat flour

Put margarine, garlic powder, brown sugar, worcestershire sauce, and oatmeal in large mixing bowl. Heat broth and pour over oatmeal, etc. Let stand five minutes. Mix well. Add egg and powdered milk and mix well. Add corn meal, mix. Mix in as much whole wheat flour as possible, then turn out and knead in enough flour so that dough does not stick to counter top. Roll to ¼" (approx.) thickness and cut into desired shapes. Bake at 300 degrees for 1 hour, then turn off oven and leave cookies inside until oven is cool.

antly, until slightly
, zucchini, oregano,

dles and bake,
for 20 minutes.

efore serving. Store
or up to 3 days.

STION: Sprinkle
zzarella cheese over
e and stir into the
eat for additional

rs of your regular
cy vet handy.
em to locate
andma Di pecially if it's an emergency!

It May *Look* Fun in the Commercials . . .

Never *ever* transport a dog (or any animal) in the back of any open pickup truck. There are so many obvious, common-sense reasons why, but if an animal absolutely *must* be transported in the back of a pickup, use a heavy-duty and well-insulated crate that is *securely* attached to the truck.

Hound Dog Hash

No need to rehash it, this is excellent for dogs
who need a temporary bland diet.

○ **Makes approximately 3 days of food for your recovering, medium-size dog** ○

We've all heard a vet say, "Go home and boil up some rice and ground meat," as a bland but palatable dish for your dog while he recovers from whatever it is that he is recovering from. We like to use chopped carrots in our dogs' dinners—they add vitamins and dogs love 'em. This dish is extremely simple, and its aroma when cooking will make you drool right along with your dog. Here's how we make it—and it never fails to encourage an ailing appetite.

4 cups long-grain rice
1 pound ground chicken or turkey
2 carrots, diced
½ cup chopped broccoli or green beans
    (optional)
1 teaspoon chopped fresh parsley

 ### For Diarrhea Relief

Try switching your dog's diet for a couple of days to a bland diet—like Hound Dog Hash. If diarrhea persists after three days, take your dog to the vet's office for further examination. Make sure your dog continues to have access to plenty of fresh, cold water to prevent dehydration during a bout of diarrhea. Use the bland diet only for short periods of time as it is not a "complete" diet.

Pour 6 cups water into a large pot and add the rice. Crumble in the ground chicken and mix well. Stir in the carrots. (You also can add a small amount of finely chopped broccoli or green beans.)

Cook over medium heat until the mixture comes to a boil. Turn the heat to low, cover, and simmer for 15 minutes. Turn off the heat and let the mixture rest for 15 minutes. (The meat and vegetables will continue to cook with the rice.)

Sprinkle parsley on top. Fluff the rice with a fork to mix the contents thoroughly.

Cool to room temperature before serving.

Store covered in the refrigerator for up to 3 days.

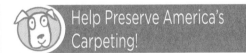

Help Preserve America's Carpeting!

Always switch your dog's diet slowly, over a period of time. Never introduce new food at a rate faster than one-seventh per day—your pooch will be completely switched over by the end of a week. An abrupt change can lead to a nasty bout of upset stomach, diarrhea, and vomiting.

¡Ay, Chihuahua! Casserole

Perfecto for dogs seeking a little
south-of-the-border collie flavor.

○ **Makes 6 servings of cha-cha-chow on a plato** ○

Rice is nice and provides a backdrop for a bit of high-energy, lower-calorie grub to keep up the stamina needed for a hard day's play. While you don't *have* to put your pooch in a Zorro mask to eat this fine dish, it can't possibly hurt. We tried putting ours in sombreros, but soon discovered that it works better if we just wear them ourselves. *Ay, ay, ay-ay* . . .

2 cups diced cooked chicken
½ cup diced carrots
2 tablespoons chopped fresh parsley
2 cups long-grain rice, cooked
½ cup skim milk
1 tablespoon all-purpose flour
1 cup shredded low-fat cheddar or mozzarella cheese

Wet Nose, Warm Heart?

A cold wet nose is not an accurate indicator of your dog's health. There are just as many reasons for a nose to be cold and wet as there are for it to be warm and dry. If your dog is not acting like herself, is coughing and sneezing, is sleeping more than usual, or is vomiting—those are true signals that she is sick.

Preheat the oven to 350°F. Grease a 9 X 13-inch baking pan with nonstick cooking spray.

Mix together the chicken, carrots, and parsley in a large bowl. Add the cooked rice and mix well. Whisk the milk and flour together in a small bowl, and pour over the rice mixture.

Place the mixture in the baking dish. Sprinkle the cheese evenly on top.

Bake for 25 to 30 minutes, or until light golden.

Cool to room temperature before serving.

Store covered in the refrigerator for up to 3 days.

 The Deep Dark Secret of Royalty and Their Lapdogs

In days gone by, members of the regal classes nearly always kept a lapdog nearby—in part to draw fleas and parasites away from their bodies!

Cluck! Cluck! Casserole

A meat-and-potatoes meal for a dog who's in a "fowl" mood.

○ Makes enough to turn any dog into a "bird" dog! ○

Picture this: It's a bone-chilling evening when you've come back dog-tired from a day in the dog-eat-dog world and just want to rest your aching dogs . . . but somebody else is dog-hungry! This casserole takes only about 10 minutes to make (5 minutes if you're full of *pup!*). It's also a great one to cook and keep in the fridge, then pop in the microwave or reheat in the oven. (Just be sure to cool before serving!) When you see the tail wags and looks of gratitude, you'll know who thinks you're top dog!

1 pound ground chicken

2 tablespoons canola oil

3 medium potatoes, sliced

3 medium carrots, sliced

1 cup long-grain rice

2 cups Homemade Chicken Stock (page 45) or canned, low-sodium chicken broth

½ cup frozen peas

¼ cup grated Parmesan cheese

Preheat the oven to 350°F. Grease a 3-quart casserole dish with nonstick cooking spray.

Cook the chicken in the oil in a sauté pan over medium heat until lightly browned.

Layer the potatoes in the casserole dish, then the carrots. Sprinkle the rice over the carrots, and pour the broth over the casserole. Spread the chicken on top of the rice. Sprinkle the peas on top of the chicken, then sprinkle with Parmesan cheese.

Bake uncovered for 1 hour.

Cool to room temperature before serving.

Store covered in the refrigerator for up to 3 days.

SALIVATIN' SERVING SUGGESTION: Ground turkey or other lean ground meats may be substituted for the chicken.

 ## Get the Massage?

Gently massage your pet (especially your older pet) every day. Your older dog will appreciate this more than she can bark. An old dog who may be full of aches and pains will enjoy the massage and the gentle pressure will help her circulation and help her feel better from tail to toe.

Entrées

Chompin' Chuck-Waggin' Chicken

A dish for spinning *tails* around the campfire—or kitchen table.

○ **Makes 4 taste-tempting servings** ○

A well-rounded all-in-one meal, filling but not heavy, this takes about five minutes of prep time. Low-fat ground chicken, along with fresh vegetables, makes this a favorite for dogs who are watching their figures—and aren't we all?

1 large potato (or two small), sliced thin
½ cup frozen peas
½ cup frozen green beans
1 pound ground chicken
1 cup skim milk
1 tablespoon all-purpose flour
Pinch of dried rosemary
Pinch of dried oregano

Preheat the oven to 375°F. Grease an 8 X 11-inch casserole dish with nonstick cooking spray.

Place half the potatoes in a layer in the bottom of the casserole dish. Sprinkle the peas and green beans evenly over the potatoes. Add another layer of potatoes. Crumble the meat on top.

Whisk the milk and flour together in a small bowl, and pour the mixture over the meat. Lightly sprinkle with rosemary and oregano.

Bake covered with aluminum foil for 30 minutes.

Cool to room temperature before serving.

Store covered in the refrigerator for up to 3 days.

SALIVATIN' SERVING SUGGESTION: Ground turkey or other lean ground meats may be substituted for the chicken.

No Bones about It

Every cartoon ever made shows a dog with a bone—or wishing he had one. As we all know, feeding bones to your dog from *any* meat source is dangerous. Bones are a choking hazard and can cause major obstructions in the digestive system or painful, even fatal, perforations in the digestive tract and bowels. Particularly dangerous are small, soft bones like chicken or pork chop bones.

Creatures of Habit

Your dog's mental outlook, security, and basic understanding of the world all may change abruptly if there is a major shift in his environment. A move to a new home, a new member added to the household, even a new schedule—anything that disrupts what he knows as his world can lead to pronounced new personality traits. During times of transition or upheaval, be sure to continue giving your dog the same or more love and attention to help him regain confidence and security.

Loafin' Dog Mutt Loaf

A definite four-paws-up favorite—and we're not kitten!

○ Makes 8 mini *mutt* loaves ○

They might be Chihuahua-size loaves, but they pack a Great Dane–size flavor. Versatile and tasty, use them as a protein-packed meal or snack—and no need to wash the plate . . . it'll be licked clean. This will have your dog grinning from ear to ear. Ears to you, kid!

1 pound ground chicken

1 large egg

1½ cups fresh bread crumbs

3 tablespoons grated Parmesan cheese

½ teaspoon dried oregano

1 teaspoon dried parsley

½ teaspoon garlic powder

Keep Things in Proportion

Think about it—a small snack to a human may translate into a large amount of calories for your dog.

Fit or Fat?

Some dog owners may not know how to tell if their dog is overweight. A simple test to see if your dog is overweight is to run your hands along his sides. You should be able to feel all the ribs with some small amount of fat layering them. Ribs that are too visible would indicate your dog is too thin. If you can't feel any ribs under the layer of fat your dog is walking around with, it's time for a diet!

Preheat the oven to 350°F. Grease a shallow baking pan with nonstick vegetable spray.

Combine all ingredients in a bowl and mix well with your hands. Shape the mixture into eight 2 X 3-inch mini loaves. Space the loaves evenly on the baking pan.

Bake for 20 minutes, or until fully cooked (155°F on an instant-read thermometer).

Cool completely before serving.

Store covered in the refrigerator for up to 3 days.

SALIVATIN' SERVING SUGGESTION: Ground turkey may be substituted for the chicken.

Weight Watchers for Dogs

If your dog is overweight (or headed in that direction), start to correct the situation by reducing his food ration each week by 10 percent. If no weight loss is evident after two weeks, you may decrease daily rations a further 10 percent. Encourage extra calorie burning by increasing your dog's activity and exercise level. (This is good for you, too!) If your dog appears to be gaining weight and you are *sure* you have not increased his food, a hormonal imbalance may be involved. Consult with your vet, who may wish to run a test for thyroid or pituitary gland dysfunction.

Entrées

Chickey Pug Pie

No other way to describe this dish . . . it's de*leash*ous!

○ Makes 12 chow-down chickey pies ○

Same Kibble, Different Day . . .

Think about it: Most people tend to feed their dogs the same thing day after day. So if the food is unhealthful and infused with chemicals and preservatives, then day after day our dogs are being exposed to those harmful and toxic agents, compounding their effects.

Don't Color Food by Number!

Colors with numbers (red 40, etc.) are inorganic, some are toxic, and *all* should be avoided. Dogs are colorblind, so manufacturers of dyed foods must think they're appealing to *us.* Do you really care about the *color* of your dog's food? We didn't think so.

Savory, wholesome, and healthy—what more could a dog want? (Except more!) Easy to prepare—what more could you want? Add your dog's favorite leftover green or yellow vegetables. Works well with leftover chopped beef or turkey, too.

2 cups minced cooked chicken (5 pulses in a food processor)

1½ cups chopped fresh veggies (green beans, carrots, peas), blanched briefly in boiling water (or one 10-ounce package frozen mixed vegetables, thawed)

1¾ cups Homemade Chicken Stock (page 45) or canned, low-sodium chicken broth

2 large eggs, slightly beaten

3 cups bread crumbs

Preheat the oven to 350°F. Grease a 12-cup muffin pan with nonstick vegetable spray.

Mix together all the ingredients in a bowl. Fill the muffin cups with the mixture, pressing down firmly.

Bake for 20 to 25 minutes, or until heated through.

Cool to room temperature before serving.

Store covered in the refrigerator for up to 3 days.

 Just Say No!

Never hit or beat your dog for destructive behaviors, even if you're tempted to. She won't make the connection, and it will only aggravate the situation and cause the anxiety to become worse. Not to mention that it's cruel.

Squirrel Stroganoff

What dog doesn't pray for the day he'll get his paws on
his eternal nemesis—the backyard squirrel?

○ **Makes 4 cups—more than enough for your little czar!** ○

OK, it's not actually squirrel, and it's not
technically a stroganoff, we just liked the
name. But when your dog gets wind that
this dish is in the oven, he's sure to come
"Russian" in!

1 tablespoon canola oil

1 pound boneless chicken, cut into ¼-inch strips

1 small baked potato, diced

2 tablespoons all-purpose flour

¾ cup Homemade Chicken Stock (see page 45), or
    canned, low-sodlum chicken broth

1 teaspoon dried parsley

½ cup low-fat or nonfat sour cream

Heat the oil in a heavy-bottomed skillet over
medium heat. Add the chicken to the skillet and
sauté until cooked through, about 5 minutes.
Stir in the potato and continue to sauté until
completely heated through.

Sprinkle the chicken mixture with the flour.
Add the chicken stock and parsley and cook
until the sauce thickens.

Cool to room temperature, stir in the sour
cream, and serve.

Store covered in the refrigerator for up
to 3 days.

SALIVATIN' SERVING SUGGESTION: Can be
served over cooked and cooled brown rice
or whole wheat pasta noodles.

The Name's "Spot"—Says So Right Here

**Always keep a collar with an up-to-date ID
tag on your dog, even when you're not out
and about with her. Pets who wear IDs have a
much greater chance of being returned if lost.**

Grandpaw's Sunday Dawg Dinner

Even the most citified critter would be happy with a heapin' helpin' of this country canine cuisine. Yee-haw!!

o **Makes about 12 small or 6 large servings—enough for a samoyed smorgasbord!** o

Over the river and through the woods . . . what young pup doesn't love to trot over to Grandpaw's for a dinner in the country? You'll have enough for an old-fashioned Sunday buffet for all the dogs in your pack—followed, of course, by the obligatory nice long Sunday afternoon snooze on the front porch.

3 pounds chicken parts
5 tablespoons all-purpose flour
One 10-ounce package frozen peas and carrots, thawed
1 teaspoon chopped fresh parsley
½ teaspoon garlic powder

Place the chicken and 3 quarts water in a stockpot. Bring to a boil and skim off the scum as it rises to the top. Turn the heat to low and simmer until the chicken is tender and cooked through, approximately 50 minutes.

Remove the chicken from the stockpot and allow to cool. Reserve the broth. When the chicken is cool enough to handle, remove and discard the skin and bones, and shred the chicken.

Whisk together ¾ cup water and the flour and stir into the chicken broth. Bring the sauce to a boil and stir until it thickens.

Preheat the oven to 350°F.

Stir into the sauce the peas and carrots, parsley, garlic powder, and reserved chicken. Pour the mixture into a 9 X 13-inch casserole dish, sprayed with nonstick vegetable spray.

Bake for 15 minutes, or until heated through.

Cool to room temperature before serving.

Store in the refrigerator for up to 3 days.

Spanish Chicken Pawella

Your dogs will trail you to *Bark*celona for some of this dish!

○ **Makes enough to turn any dog into the Dog of "La Muncha"** ○

Spaniels are thought to have originated in Spain, so it's only appropriate to include a recipe from the Iberian peninsula. Or as our neighbor's husky puts it, the "Siberian" peninsula. We love this recipe because: (a) it's not your typical paella; (b) it's loaded with vitamins, fiber, carbohydrates, and protein; and (c) our dogs can't get enough of it.

4 tablespoons canola oil
2 pounds boneless chicken breasts or thighs, cut into 1-inch cubes
2 cups long-grain rice
1 pound sweet potatoes, diced
1½ cups frozen peas
1½ cups chopped fresh tomatoes
1 teaspoon dried oregano
½ teaspoon garlic powder
¼ cup chopped fresh parsley
4 cups Homemade Chicken Stock (page 45), or canned, low-sodium chicken broth

Heat the oil in a large skillet over medium heat. Add the chicken and cook until lightly browned. Add the rice, sweet potatoes, peas, tomatoes, oregano, garlic powder, and parsley. Cook for 1 minute, stirring constantly. Add the chicken stock and bring to a boil, then lower the heat and simmer for 20 minutes, covered, until the rice is tender.

Cool to room temperature before serving.

Store covered in the refrigerator for up to 3 days.

The "C" Word

Nobody likes to think about cancer, in themselves or in the ones they love. Sadly, our dogs are just as susceptible to cancer as we are. Luckily, the earlier we spot signs of it, the better the chances of doing something about it. Here are the common signs of cancer in dogs:

- o Abnormal persistent swelling of an area
- o Sores that do not heal
- o Unexplained weight loss
- o Loss of appetite
- o Bleeding from any body opening
- o Offensive odor (we're not talking about your dog's normal bad breath!)

- o Difficulty eating or swallowing
- o Loss of stamina
- o Lameness
- o Reluctance to exercise
- o Difficulty urinating or defecating
- o Difficulty breathing

If you see *any* of these signs, *please* call your vet—don't wait until it's too late!

Dish-'Em-Up Dumplings

You know life is good when there's lickin' and chicken!

○ **Makes several bellyfuls, depending on the size of your dog's tummy** ○

You'll barely have to lift a paw to put this salivatingly sensational dish together. Fetch some extra vegetables to simmer in the broth to add an additional *bone*us: more flavor and more vitamins. "Dig" through your fridge . . . but remember: only *fresh* vegetables, nothing wilted or moldy.

1 quart Homemade Chicken Stock (page 45), or canned, low-sodium chicken broth
1 cup all-purpose flour
½ cup fresh bread crumbs
2 teaspoons baking powder
1 large egg, beaten
2 tablespoons canola oil
⅓ cup skim milk
1 tablespoon minced fresh parsley
2 boneless chicken breasts, cubed

Bring the chicken stock to a boil in a medium pot and then reduce to a simmer. Meanwhile, combine the flour, bread crumbs, and baking powder in a bowl and set aside. In a large bowl, beat together the egg, oil, and milk. Stir in the dry ingredients and the parsley to make a stiff batter.

Add the chicken to the broth. Drop the batter by the tablespoonful into the broth. Cover and steam for 20 minutes without removing the cover.

Cool to room temperature. Serve the dumplings with some of the boneless diced chicken and broth.

Store covered in the refrigerator for up to 3 days.

What's Up, Doc?

Your dog may enjoy gnawing on a raw carrot. It will also help clean his teeth and massage his gums, increasing circulation in the oral cavity.

It's Easy Eating Green

Most dogs thoroughly enjoy vegetables, especially carrots, squash, green beans, zucchini, and broccoli—and they're good for them, too! Adding a small amount of veggies to your dog's dinner will add nutrients, vitamins, and minerals, and *ruff*age to her system. For proper digestion, cook broccoli and green beans before feeding them to your dog. P.S. Always make sure you thoroughly wash fresh vegetables and fruits before giving them to your pet. Even better, use organic produce whenever possible for your own well-being, too.

Bird and Barley Savory Snarf Down

Magic! Serve up a plate and watch your dog turn into a pig.

○ Makes 4 to 6 personal feeding frenzies for your dog ○

Man's Best (and Oldest) Friend

The oldest evidence science has produced of dogs as companion animals is a 14,000-year-old fossilized specimen found in an Iraqi cave.

What makes the death suspicious is the presence of what looks like prehistoric kibble nearby—uneaten!

Did you know nutritious whole-grain barley is one of the world's oldest grains? In ancient times, it was commonly used to feed animals and pets. That makes this one of the world's oldest and newest recipes at the same time.

3 tablespoons canola oil
1 cup pearled barley
½ cup diced carrots
¼ cup diced celery
½ cup frozen chopped spinach, thawed and
    drained
1 cup shredded cooked chicken
3 cups Homemade Chicken Stock (page 45), or
    canned, low-sodium chicken broth, boiling
½ teaspoon dried oregano
½ teaspoon dried basil
½ teaspoon garlic powder

Heat the oil over medium-high heat in a large saucepan. Add the barley. Stir to coat with oil until lightly toasted, about 1 minute. Add the carrots, celery, spinach, and cooked chicken, stirring for 1 minute. Then add the chicken stock, oregano, basil, and garlic powder.

Cover and simmer for 25 minutes.

Cool to room temperature before serving.

Store covered in the refrigerator for up to 3 days.

Now *That's* a Pedigree

Lore holds that there were two dogs on the *Mayflower* when it arrived in 1620: a mastiff and a cocker spaniel.

According to *official* reports, they were "just good friends."

Those Mandatory Sentencing Laws

Pekinese were considered sacred in ancient China and were the dogs of the emperor's court. Anyone found harming a Pekinese could be punished by death.

Even the few thugs who *wanted* to hurt a peekie must have thought twice before actually doing it. Wouldn't it be nice if everyone who had the impulse to hurt *any* dog did the same?

Roamin' Holiday

A dish that will inspire drooly dreams from your little vege*terrier*.

○ Makes 8 servings of cheesy, chewy *Itail*ian amore ○

There'll be no more roamin' from the food dish once you try this Roman classic. This is what we call some good ciao.

One 28-ounce can crushed tomatoes
One 10-ounce package frozen chopped spinach,
    thawed and drained
1 teaspoon dried oregano
12 ounces rigatoni pasta, cooked and drained
½ cup grated Parmesan cheese
¼ cup grated mozzarella cheese
½ cup grated provolone cheese

Preheat oven to 350°F. Grease a 9 X 13-inch baking pan with nonstick vegetable spray.

Mix together the tomatoes, spinach, and oregano in a large bowl. Add the pasta and toss well. Add the Parmesan cheese and toss again.

Spread the pasta mixture evenly in the baking pan. Sprinkle the top of the casserole with mozzarella and provolone cheeses, and cover with aluminum foil.

Bake for 25 minutes. Remove the foil and bake 10 minutes longer, or until the cheese is bubbling and lightly browned on top.

Cool to room temperature before serving.

Store covered in the refrigerator for up to 3 days.

Hey, Dog Breath!

A raw, finely minced carrot mixed with a sprinkling of minced fresh parsley and finely chopped fresh mint leaves will help your dog's bad breath.

Separation Anxiety

Separation anxiety is a panicky behavior exhibited by certain dogs when left alone. The syndrome is genuine panic, not your dog throwing a "fit" or acting up just to teach you a lesson. Some dogs suffer severe bouts of separation anxiety while others show no signs whatsoever.

There are many reasons why separation anxiety can occur, but basically it happens to dogs who are left alone and can't cope with your not being there with them. Any abrupt and disruptive change in the household's environment has the potential to trigger separation anxiety.

If your dog shows signs of separation anxiety (these might include going to the bathroom inside the house, chewing furniture and rugs, knocking over the trash, signs of depression as you prepare to leave, etc.), some experts recommend you try these methods:

o Leave home quietly without all the "Oh, bye-bye, my baby. Ohhhhh, I'm gonna go to worky now . . . bye-bye . . . come give Mommy a kiss." Just leave. Don't make a scene every time you come and go.

o Leave a piece or two of clothing with your scent still lingering on it on the floor, where your dog can lie on it (but not your favorite blouse—just in case).

o Leave a radio or TV on low volume.

o Leave out a couple of safe toys or treats.

o Practice leaving your dog for just a few moments, then come back into the house without paying attention to him. Make these "practice" absences longer and longer.

Just Dogserts

Ah, what better way to top off an evening than with a little barking over a dessert plate? Our dessert recipes contain no white sugar, although some call for a bit of honey or molasses as a natural sweetener for your natural sweetie. Whether you're preparing Dottie's Spots, Belly Rub Brownies, or Yip-Yap Banana Snaps, you know your dogs are going to snap into full tail-wag mode over what's wafting out of the oven—so be sure to make extra. Drop a batch or two off at your local animal shelter and enjoy some good karma as a *bone*us for your efforts. Happy baking—and barking!

Happy Hound Cake

This is the snack for all the occasions when
your hound is, well, happy.

○ Makes 1 cake; *paw*tion size varies depending on the size of your hound ○

Lots of reasons for an impromptu shindig: graduation from obedience school, welcome home from the kennel, first visit to the vet—or simply an I'm-glad-we-found-each-other moment. Definitely a recipe worthy of our coveted 10-Lick Best of Dining Award.

1¾ cup all-purpose flour
½ cup carob powder (available at health food stores)
1 teaspoon baking powder
½ cup canola oil
1 cup honey
4 large egg whites
1 cup plain nonfat yogurt
1 teaspoon pure vanilla extract

Preheat the oven to 350°F. Grease an 8- or 9-inch round cake pan with nonstick vegetable spray and dust with flour.

Stir together the flour, carob powder, and baking powder in a bowl and set aside. In a large bowl, mix the oil and honey with an electric mixer or wooden spoon. Add the egg whites, one at a time, continuing to beat. Add the yogurt and vanilla and mix to combine thoroughly. Add the dry ingredients to the wet ingredients and mix until smooth.

 I'm Not Bored—Really!

Current wisdom holds that a dog's yawn is not a sign of boredom, but of peace and contentment!

Spread the batter evenly in the cake pan. Bake for 30 to 35 minutes, or until a toothpick inserted in the center of the cake comes out clean.

Cool to room temperature before serving.

Store in an airtight container for up to 3 days, or wrap well and freeze for up to 2 months. (Thaw before serving.)

Insect Gourmets

For maximum dining pleasure, an insect often bites the areas of your dog with the least fur. If you notice extra licking or itching around the belly, paws, nose, or ears, be sure to see what's going on in those areas. Catching a bite or infection early can make a big difference in the treatment and healing process.

Quality Time

Dogs who must spend inordinate amounts of time alone become depressed, lonely, bored, and destructive. Consider enrolling your dog in day care or hiring someone to come in and play with her a few times a week. Perhaps think about getting a pet for your pet! A second dog will provide companionship and stimulation to a home-alone dog. In any event, be sure to spend a good, solid amount of time each and every day with your dog.

Apple Cinnamon Fetch 'Ems

An apple a day keeps the vet away. . . .

○ **Makes 12 happy, snappy apple treats** ○

Over 7,500 varieties of apples are grown throughout the world—from the size of a cherry to as large as a grapefruit—and dogs seem to love 'em all. They make the perfect dessert for those chilly autumn nights. Also those warm spring afternoons. Not to mention those sultry summer mornings. Winter around dusk isn't too bad, either. . . .

1½ cups all-purpose flour
1½ cups whole wheat flour
1 tablespoon baking powder
1 teaspoon ground cinnamon
¾ cup honey
2 cups unsweetened applesauce
½ cup canola oil
2 large eggs
½ cup skim milk

Preheat the oven to 350°F. Grease a 12-cup muffin pan with nonstick vegetable spray.

Stir together the flours, baking powder, and cinnamon in a large bowl and set aside. In a separate bowl, whisk together the honey, applesauce, and oil. Then whisk in the eggs one at a time. Add the milk and continue whisking. Add the wet ingredients to the dry ingredients and stir just until combined.

Fill the muffin cups ⅔ full. Bake for 30 minutes, or until a toothpick inserted in the center of a muffin comes out clean.

Cool to room temperature before serving.

Store in an airtight container for up to 4 days, or wrap well and freeze for up to 2 months. (Thaw before serving.)

 The Name Game

Although no two lists anywhere match exactly, top dog names in the United States definitely include:

o Sam	o Buddy	o Ginger
o Max	o Tasha	o Jake
o Lady	o Chelsea	o Lucy
o Bear	o Holly	o Daisy
o Maggie		

Top lists even vary geographically, with dogs in the Midwest having the most food-related names, like Taffy, Pepsi, or Meatball.

Grrrrrrnola Muttins

Granola, the hippie food of the 1960s,
is now the "yippy" food of the new millennium.

○ **Makes 24 tune-in, turn-on, drop-out mutt muffins. Peace.** ○

What's the Frequency, Fido?

Your dog can definitely pick up on the "vibe" in your home's environment. Dogs connect with the energy that we send out—since we haven't learned to speak Dog, they've learned to read us emotionally. Our tone of voice, posture, expressions, and mood all play into a pet's ability to communicate with us. Angry people sometimes create angry dogs. Calm people, calm dogs.

Close your eyes, and repeat: I am one with my biscuits, I am one with my biscuits . . .

This recipe has practically limitless whisker-licking potential—pears, peaches, or bananas can be substituted for apples, and your local health food store stocks a plethora of granola flavors. You can do the math, but you'll need all four paws to count the flavor possibilities.

2 cups all-purpose flour
1 cup quick rolled oats
1½ cups unsweetened granola (NO RAISINS!)
2 tablespoons baking powder
1 teaspoon ground cinnamon
1 cup honey
½ cup canola oil
2 large eggs
1 large apple, diced (about 1 cup)

GCGGRRR RRRR

GRRRRRRR

Preheat the oven to 400°F. Grease two 12-cup muffin pans with nonstick vegetable spray.

Stir together the flour, oats, granola, baking powder, and cinnamon in a large bowl and set aside. In a separate bowl, whisk together the honey and oil. Whisk in the eggs, one at a time, then 1¼ cups water. Add the wet ingredients to the dry ingredients and stir just until combined. Fold in the apples or the fruit of your choice.

Fill the muffin cups ⅔ full. Bake for 20 to 25 minutes, or until a toothpick inserted in the center of a muffin comes out clean.

Cool to room temperature before serving.

Store in an airtight container for up to 4 days, or wrap well and freeze for up to 2 months. (Thaw before serving.)

 ## Hey, Dude, Got Any Grass?

Dogs sometimes eat grass when outside. This does not necessarily mean your dog is sick or trying to vomit. It may merely indicate that your dog likes grass. If your dog *loves* to eat grass, keep him away from all grass that has been treated with pesticides, herbicides, and/or fertilizers. That would include *all* lawns that look perfect or even just weed-free.

Just *Dogserts*

Labrador Love "Bites"

Satisfies even the hairiest hound's sweet fang.

o **Makes 36 fun-to-nibble minicakes** o

We haven't found a Labrador—or any dog, for that matter—who wouldn't trade the neighbor's cat to chomp on this tasty treat. With velvety smooth honey and all-natural carob (carob, unlike chocolate, is fine for dogs), this is a naturally sweet treat for your little honey. Bake extra and throw a few in the freezer for thawing out during the hot dog days of summer.

2½ cups all-purpose flour

¾ teaspoon baking powder

½ teaspoon ground cinnamon

2 tablespoons carob powder (available at health food stores)

½ cup honey

½ cup canola oil

2 large eggs

¾ cup unsweetened applesauce

½ cup carob chips (available at health food stores)

Preheat the oven to 325°F. Grease three 12-cup mini-muffin pans with nonstick vegetable spray.

Stir together the flour, baking powder, cinnamon, and carob powder in a large bowl and set aside. In a separate bowl, whisk together the honey and oil. Add the eggs, one at a time, then the applesauce, whisking thoroughly after each addition. Add the wet ingredients to the dry ingredients and stir just until moistened.

Fill the mini-muffin cups ⅔ full. Sprinkle with the carob chips and bake for 20 to 25 minutes, or until a toothpick inserted in the center of a muffin comes out clean.

Cool to room temperature before serving.

Store in an airtight container for up to 4 days, or wrap well and freeze for up to 2 months. (Thaw before serving.)

 ## Creepy, Crawly Creatures

Dogs love nothing more than sniffing around through brush and tall grasses, and because of that they are prone to being bitten by ticks, spiders, and snakes. Take the time to educate yourself about the hazards that exist in your geographic area and learn how to deal with it if danger should strike your dog.

 ## Tick, Tick, Tick . . .

Ticks are like little time bombs—their germs can transmit Lyme disease to your dog a long time after the bite, so check your dog thoroughly after any good outside romp. If you check for ticks often, you will greatly reduce the chance of your dog getting Lyme disease, since a tick must be attached to your dog for a full day before the disease is transmitted. Signs of Lyme disease are lethargy, fever, and swollen, painful joints. If you have any fears that your dog may have contracted Lyme disease, take him in your vet at once.

Just Dogserts

Belly-Rub Brownies

Besides all the tail-chasing, there are the tennis balls to fetch, the mailman to scare, the cat to chase, the sofa to chew . . .

○ **Makes 16 un*fur*gettably de*leash*ous bar cookies** ○

A dog's work is never done, it seems. However, Claire knows how to relax and has *us* well trained. She loves to eat one of these brownies and then go lie on her back with all four paws in the air in the hope that we'll come over to rub her

No Strings

Don't let your dog play with string or any toys that can unravel into long threadlike parts. String, thread, yarn, and other materials can become entwined around your dog's intestines. Should you see any sign of string coming out either end of your dog, take her to the vet at once. Do not attempt to pull the string out as it may be entwined around internal organs.

belly. And, of course, we do. Dog-friendly carob is naturally low in fat and high in calcium and fiber. (Claire likes it when we mash a banana into the batter, too.)

1¼ cups all-purpose flour
3 tablespoons carob powder (available at health food stores)
½ teaspoon baking powder
½ cup canola oil
¾ cup honey
2 large eggs

Preheat the oven to 350°F. Grease an 8-inch square baking pan with nonstick vegetable spray.

Stir together the flour, carob powder, and baking powder in a large bowl and set aside. In a small bowl, whisk together the oil and honey.

Add the eggs, one at a time, whisking to incorporate. Add the wet ingredients to the dry ingredients and stir until well blended.

Spread the batter evenly in the pan. Bake for 20 to 25 minutes, or until the brownies start to pull away from the sides of the pan.

Cool to room temperature, cut into bars, and serve.

Store in an airtight container for up to 4 days, or wrap well and freeze for up to 2 months. (Thaw before serving.)

Another Reason to Pick Up Your Panty Hose

Puppies *love* to chew panty hose! They also love socks and other small undergarments. Puppies are attracted to such *paw*sonal items because, well, they smell like you. Panty hose are particularly dangerous as they can become entwined in the digestive tract. As odd as it sounds, removing swallowed panty hose is a common reason for emergency surgery.

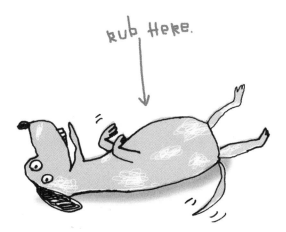

rub Here.

Spots

Dottie says, "Serve 'em up four at a time—one for each paw!"

○ **Makes 3 dozen cookies—spotted, just like Dottie!** ○

We love this recipe—and so does our Dalmatian Dottie, for obvious reasons. Fresh-baked to a golden finish—with just a touch of honey—Spots are *paw*fect for any occasion. Try them as a bath bribe to entice "Dirty Hairy" to the tub or simply when your pup is jonesin' for bones.

3 cups all-purpose flour
¾ teaspoon baking powder
1 cup molasses
1 cup canola oil
2 large eggs
1 tablespoon pure vanilla extract
One 12-ounce package carob chips (available at health food stores)

Preheat the oven to 350°F.

Stir together the flour and baking powder in a bowl and set aside. In a large bowl, whisk together the molasses and oil. Add the eggs, one at a time, and the vanilla. Stir the dry ingredients into the wet ingredients, then stir in the carob chips.

Drop the dough by the rounded teaspoonful, 1½ inches apart, on ungreased baking sheets. Bake for 12 to 14 minutes, or until light golden.

Cool completely before serving.

Store in an airtight container for up to 1 week, or wrap well and freeze for up to 2 months. (Thaw before serving.)

Heard about the Latest Hot Spot?

Unfortunately, it's not a nightclub catering to a canine clientele. Hot spots are one of your dog's most common enemies. They can be caused in several ways, including flea infestations (or even single bites), an insect sting, an allergic reaction, or a scraping of the skin against a rough edge such as fencing. A bored dog who licks himself can create a hot spot. The area may start out red and inflamed and end up as a bleeding, oozing, infected mess. You may have to shave around the infected area before cleaning thoroughly. Elizabethan collars are uncomfortable for dogs, but will keep them from licking the area and give it an opportunity to clear up. Try using an over-the-counter topical antibacterial cream. (Call your vet for a recommendation.) If the area does not begin to improve, consult your vet for something stronger—but help your pet get rid of his hot spots!

Just Dogserts

Banana Oat Woofles

Dogs love to wolf down their Woofles!

o Makes 3 dozen wolf-'em-down wonders o

The only problem with this recipe is that it's just too good—not a single dog in our mongrel horde will take the time to savor the subtlety of the cinnamon or relish the exquisite bouquet of the vanilla as it wafts through the kitchen and up the stairs into their private chambers. Oh, no, they just want to pop them like pills, the more, the faster, the better. Fine. So be it. Maybe *some*day they'll appreciate us. In the meantime, with ingredients this tasty, they sure *oat* to be good!

1½ cups all-purpose flour
¼ teaspoon baking powder
¾ teaspoon ground cinnamon
1½ cups quick rolled oats
¾ cup canola oil
½ cup honey
1 large egg
2 medium ripe bananas, mashed
1 tablespoon pure vanilla extract

Preheat the oven to 400°F. Grease 2 baking sheets with nonstick vegetable spray.

Stir together the flour, baking powder, cinnamon, and oats in a bowl and set aside. In a large bowl, using an electric mixer on low

 Sneeze or Snooze

Keep your dog off the couch by sprinkling a little pepper on it.

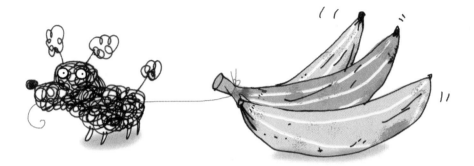

speed, mix the oil, honey, egg, bananas, and vanilla until thoroughly combined. Stir the dry ingredients into the wet ingredients.

Drop the dough by the rounded teaspoonful, 2 inches apart, on the baking sheets. Bake for 12 to 15 minutes, or until light golden.

Cool to room temperature before serving.

Store in an airtight container for up to 1 week, or wrap well and freeze for up to 2 months. (Thaw before serving.)

Was That the Dog? Okay, That Was Definitely the Dog . . .

Doggie flatulence—sorry to bring it up—is commonly caused by a dog inhaling or gulping air into the stomach while eating. If your dog is an out-of-control snarfer at the food bowl, some vets recommend placing a large rock or brick in the bowl, to force the dog to eat slower and around the brick. Sometimes this method can cure the problem. You might also try feeding your superfast eater from a 12-portion muffin pan—the small amount of food in each muffin area is bound to slow things down. And not a moment too soon.

Healing Herbs

With all the advances in medical science, it's easy to forget that for centuries we've had natural "medicines" in the herbs around us—and it's easy to forget that those herbal remedies still work! Here is a handful we use all the time:

o **Aloe vera**—Aloe vera is very easily grown, even in apartments, and is a proven soothing agent for cuts, scrapes, burns, rashes, and stings. Simply break the stem off an aloe vera plant and rub the plant directly on the affected area.

o **Apple cider vinegar**—Apple cider vinegar is helpful for clearing up chronic yeast infections of the ear. Dilute 1 teaspoon in ½ glass water, then use to swab out the infected ear; the acidity kills the yeast.

o **Chamomile**—Brew a calming tea to help induce relaxation and reduce stress in humans and pets, too. Let the tea cool completely, and serve it to your dog. Some vets say it is effective in calming an anxious dog. Tea can be diluted with additional water, if necessary. Tea should not replace fresh drinking water.

o **Kelp**—A type of seaweed available in powdered form in most health food stores, kelp is rich in iodine, a mineral that helps support thyroid function. (The thyroid helps control metabolism.) Consult your vet for the dosage appropriate for your dog.

o **Tea tree oil**—An antifungal and antibacterial extract, tea tree oil can be useful in treating flea and other bites or minor cuts and scrapes. Read package information well and consult your vet for more information.

Very Berry Drooly Dreams

Blueberries are the perfect treat to chase away the blues.

○ **Makes 1 dozen berry, berry good cakes** ○

Let's face it: Dogs will have their cake and eat it, too. And the only thing better than a blueberry Drooly Dream is 12 of them! Double the recipe and you'll have enough to share with even the biggest dogs on the block.

1¼ cups all-purpose flour
1 cup quick rolled oats
1 tablespoon baking powder
¼ cup canola oil
½ cup honey
2 large eggs
½ cup low-fat sour cream
½ cup skim milk
1 cup blueberries, fresh or frozen and thawed

Preheat the oven to 375°F. Grease a 12-cup muffin pan with nonstick vegetable spray.

Stir together the flour, oats, and baking powder in a large bowl and set aside. In a separate bowl, whisk together the oil and honey. Add the eggs, one at a time, then the sour cream and milk. Add the wet ingredients to the dry ingredients and stir just until moistened. Fold in the blueberries.

Fill the muffin cups ⅔ full and bake for 30 minutes, or until a toothpick inserted in the center of a muffin comes out clean.

Cool the cakes to room temperature before serving.

Store in an airtight container for up to 3 days, or wrap well and freeze for up to 2 months. (Thaw before serving.)

Just Dogserts

Best-in-Show Brownies

The dessert of champions!

○ **Makes 16 blue-ribbon brownies** ○

The judges have made it *arf*ficial—these brownies take first prize. Which is perfect, because your dog is a real champion. The frosting on this dessert is you don't have to have a pedigree to enjoy it!

 ## The Tall and the Small of It

Chihuahuas are the smallest breed recognized by the AKC, and Irish wolfhounds are the tallest.

¼ cup canola oil

3½ tablespoons carob powder (available at health food stores)

1 cup honey

½ cup plain nonfat yogurt

2 large eggs, beaten

1 tablespoon pure vanilla extract

2½ cups all-purpose flour

1 teaspoon baking powder

Frosting (recipe follows)

Preheat the oven to 325°F. Grease an 8-inch square baking pan with nonstick vegetable spray.

Combine the oil and carob powder with 1 cup water in a large saucepan, stir to mix, and bring to a boil. Remove from the heat and let cool to room temperature.

Whisk in the honey, yogurt, eggs, and vanilla. Stir in the flour and baking powder.

Spread the batter evenly in the pan. Bake for 30 to 35 minutes, or until brownies start to pull away from the sides of the pan.

Cool to room temperature. Prepare the frosting, frost, cut into squares, and serve.

Store in the refrigerator for up to 5 days, or wrap well and freeze for up to 2 months. (Thaw before serving.)

Frosting

One 8-ounce package low-fat cream cheese, softened

3 tablespoons carob powder (available at health food stores)

1 tablespoon pure vanilla extract

Combine all ingredients in a bowl and beat until smooth.

 Who's in First?

The AKC's coveted most popular *spot* changes over the years. Cocker spaniels ranked number 1 from 1940 to 1952, until they were usurped (or is that us*lurp*ed?) by beagles from 1953 to 1959. Poodles came in at number 1 from 1960 to 1983—a full 23 years in a row! Cockers reclaimed the throne from 1984 to 1990, and then Labradors began the reign that continues to this day.

Just *Dogserts*

Greyhound Gobbler Cobbler

Your hound will "SIT!" and "STAY!"
for a chance to gobble a few—guaranteed!

o **Makes 48 greyhound-thin dessert squares** o

Cinnamon, once used in ancient love potions, and honey, the world's original sweetener, are a perfect pairing. This is a simple recipe and easy technique but provides a rich, complex flavor. These aromatic pooch pleasers disappear faster than a speeding greyhound!

1½ cups all-purpose flour
¼ teaspoon baking powder
2 teaspoons ground cinnamon
¼ cup chopped unsalted peanuts
¾ cup honey

Preheat the oven to 350°F. Grease a baking sheet with nonstick vegetable spray.

Stir together the flour, baking soda, cinnamon, and peanuts in a bowl and set aside. Whisk the honey with ¼ cup water in a large bowl. Add the dry ingredients to the honey mixture and stir to form a smooth dough.

Place the dough on a lightly floured surface and, with a rolling pin, roll it out to approximately ⅛-inch thickness. Cut into 1-inch squares and place on the baking sheet. Bake for 12 to 15 minutes, or until light golden in color.

Cool to room temperature before serving.

Store in an airtight container for up to 1 week, or wrap well and freeze for up to 2 months. (Thaw before serving.)

 Mealtime Etiquette

If you have multiple dogs, make sure you are present while they are eating to prevent the dominant dog from greedily gulping down the lesser dog's food.

 Leader of the Pack

Dogs are pack animals, and the leader of their pack is known as the alpha dog. A dog's pack instinct makes her either lead or follow. It is important that you establish yourself as the alpha dog in your household's pack, or you will not be respected or obeyed. To be identified as the alpha dog, make sure your commands are obeyed before offering any reward or praise. You decide when playtime is over. Make your dog obey (for example, "sit" before being served dinner). Examine your dog's feet, ears, and belly and open her mouth to look in several times a week, just to reinforce the idea that *you* are in charge—not her. A household where the dog thinks she is alpha is always a bad idea for everyone involved.

Salivatin' Cinnamon Apple Nips

Now the furry little apple of your eye
will have yet another reason to love you.

○ **Makes 30 cookies—enough for the whole litter!** ○

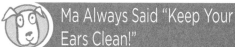

Ma Always Said "Keep Your Ears Clean!"

Floppy ears are naturally susceptible to bacteria growth, potentially leading to ear infection or even deafness. Bacteria love dark, moist, warm areas to breed in. If your dog has floppy ears, check them often.

Apples and whole oats sweetened with a touch of honey and a sprinkle of cinnamon will definitely get your pooch's full ears-up attention. They make a great reward for your pup just for being so darn cute!

1 cup all-purpose flour
1 cup quick rolled oats
1 teaspoon baking powder
1 teaspoon ground cinnamon
½ cup canola oil
⅓ cup honey
2 eggs
1 cup cored and diced apple

Preheat the oven to 350°F. Grease 2 baking sheets with nonstick vegetable spray.

Stir together the flour, oats, baking powder, and cinnamon in a bowl and set aside. In a large bowl, stir together the oil and honey until well blended. Add the eggs, one at a time, stirring to combine. Add the dry ingredients to the egg mixture and stir to form a smooth dough. Fold in the apples.

Drop the dough by the rounded teaspoonful, 1½ inches apart, on the baking sheets. Bake for 12 to 15 minutes, or until light golden.

Cool to room temperature before serving.

Store in an airtight container for up to 1 week, or wrap well and freeze for up to 2 months. (Thaw before serving.)

 ## A Dab'll Do Ya

Some veterinarians recommend using monthly or seasonal topical treatments to control fleas and ticks. Usually a few drops are applied on the dog's skin, between the shoulder blades. Such treatments are extremely easy to apply and generally are very effective in controlling parasites. However, they are difficult to remove if your pet does have a reaction, and you should keep small children away from the pet for up to 48 hours while the treatment is settling in. Ask your own vet for a brand recommendation.

Yip Yap Banana Snaps

Dogs hang around in bunches waiting for one.

o **Makes approximately 36 cookies—enough to fill a doggie bag!** o

Bananas really ap*peel* to dogs. They're chockful of potassium, fiber, vitamins A, B, and C, calcium, magnesium—hmmm, we should eat more of them, too! When bananas, oats, and honey are combined—it's a beautiful thing.

1½ cups all-purpose flour
½ teaspoon baking soda
¾ teaspoon ground cinnamon
¾ cup canola oil
2 to 3 large ripe bananas, mashed
½ cup honey
1 large egg
1¾ cup quick rolled oats

Preheat the oven to 400°F.

Stir together the flour, baking soda, and cinnamon in a large bowl. Stir in the oil, bananas, honey, and egg until smooth. Fold in the oats.

Drop the dough by the rounded teaspoonful, 1½ inches apart, on 2 ungreased baking sheets. Bake 12 to 15 minutes, or until light golden.

Cool to room temperature before serving.

Store in an airtight container for up to 1 week, or wrap well and freeze for up to 2 months. (Thaw before serving.)

The "Fix" Is In

Spaying and neutering your pets helps them live longer and healthier lives. In addition, fixing them greatly reduces the incidence of various cancers: breast cancer, testicular cancer, prostate disease—and, of course, unwanted pregnancies. It's best to spay or neuter before six months of age.

Peanut Mutter Nibbles

Peanut butter is a perfectly tasty way to indulge your little nut.

○ Makes 3 dozen peanutty paw pleasers ○

We ask you: What dog would bark "no" to peanut butter? None whom we know! The classic pairing of honey with peanut butter will have your dogs hypnotized in drooly, zombielike anticipation. Repeat after us: You are getting hungry . . . you are getting very, very hungry. . . .

3½ cups all-purpose flour
1 teaspoon baking powder
2 tablespoons canola oil
1 cup honey
¼ cup unsalted peanut butter
2 large eggs
1 teaspoon pure vanilla extract

Preheat the oven to 350°F.

Stir together the flour and baking powder in a bowl and set aside. Cream together the oil, honey, peanut butter, and vanilla in a large bowl. Add the eggs, one at a time, stirring to incorporate. Add the dry ingredients to the wet ingredients and stir to form a smooth dough.

Drop the dough by the rounded teaspoonful, 1½ inches apart, on 2 ungreased baking sheets. Bake for 12 to 14 minutes, or until light golden.

Cool completely before serving.

Store in an airtight container for up to 1 week, or wrap well and freeze for up to 2 months. (Thaw before serving.)

A Few More Words and They Can Get Their GED!

Some scholars and dog trainers believe an average canine can distinguish and comprehend up to 200 words.

95

Encore Apple Cake

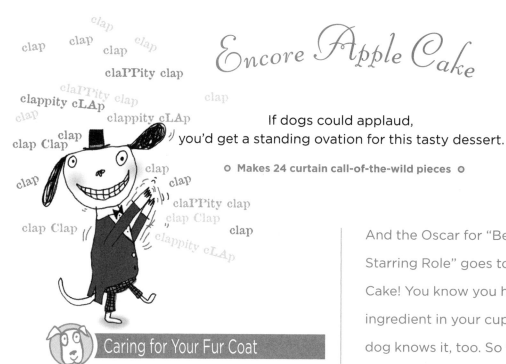

clap clap clap clap clap claPPity clap clappity cLAp claPPity clap clap clap clappity cLAp clap clap Clap clap clap clap claPPity clap clap Clap clap clap Clap clappity cLAp

If dogs could applaud,
you'd get a standing ovation for this tasty dessert.

◦ Makes 24 curtain call-of-the-wild pieces ◦

Caring for Your Fur Coat

Rubbing ice on your dog's fur will sometimes harden sticky items like gum that your dog may lie or roll in, making it easier to remove. Working vegetable or olive oil into a sticky mess in your dog's fur can help break up and remove sticky substances, too. Afterward be sure to wipe any residue off thoroughly with a warm wet towel. Never ever use paint thinners, adhesive solvents, or chemical removers on your dog's fur or skin. Such solvents can be absorbed through the skin, causing kidney or liver damage.

And the Oscar for "Best Recipe in a Starring Role" goes to Encore Apple Cake! You know you have every single ingredient in your cupboard—and your dog knows it, too. So why don't you give in and get busy baking? Luscious sweet apple, combined with whole oats and molasses—all we can say is: Lights! Action! Munch!

2 cups all-purpose flour

½ cup quick rolled oats

2 teaspoons baking powder

2 teaspoons ground cinnamon

6 tablespoons canola oil

¾ cup molasses

1¾ cup unsweetened applesauce

1 large egg

1 teaspoon pure vanilla extract

1 apple, cored and chopped (about 1 cup)

Preheat the oven to 350°F.

Grease and flour a 13 X 9-inch baking pan.

Stir together the flour, oats, baking powder, and cinnamon in a bowl and set aside. In a large bowl, stir together the oil, molasses, applesauce, egg, and vanilla. Add the dry ingredients to the wet ingredients and mix just enough to form a smooth batter. Fold in the apple.

Spread the batter evenly in the pan. Bake for 25 to 35 minutes, or until a toothpick inserted in the center of the cake comes out clean. Cut into 24 bars.

Cool completely before serving.

Store in an airtight container for up to 5 days, or wrap well and freeze for up to 2 months. (Thaw before serving.)

Can't You Hear What I'm Not Saying?

Dogs communicate with us and with each other through their facial expressions, body postures, tail and ear positioning, and barking patterns. Much as we enjoy canine charades, wouldn't it be nice if every once in a while they would just come right out and say what they mean?

Mongrel Munchers

A wholesome, all-natural treat for your wholesome, all-natural dog!

○ **Makes about 20 mutt pleasers—double it for twice the tail wags!** ○

Not only are these cookies delicious, the recipe is so darn simple, it almost makes itself . . . we barely have to lift a paw. For years we've used variations of this recipe—whether for a TV baking spot or a Humane Society fundraiser. Whip up a batch today and let the munching begin!

1 cup all-purpose flour
2 cups quick rolled oats
½ cup chopped unsalted peanuts
1 large ripe banana, mashed
¼ cup unsweetened applesauce
½ teaspoon pure vanilla extract

Preheat the oven to 350°F.

Stir together the flour, oats, and peanuts in a bowl and set aside. In a large bowl, stir together the banana, applesauce, and vanilla. Add the dry ingredients to the banana mixture and stir to form a stiff dough.

Roll the dough into walnut-size balls and flatten on an ungreased baking sheet with the back of a spoon or your hand. Bake for 15 minutes, or until light golden.

Cool on a rack completely before serving.

Store in an airtight container for up to 1 week, or wrap well and freeze for up to 2 months. (Thaw before serving.)

Well, I Joined the Gym after New Year's, But . . .

Every dog needs and enjoys exercise, but not all dogs are equipped for *vigorous* exercise. Start slow and build from there. Be sensitive to your own dog's limitations, factoring in age, weight, and general health. Even if your old dog is throbbing with painful arthritis, he'll still want to try to jog alongside you just to be with you. It's your job to say no.

That's Why They Keep Jumping on the Couch

Tests conducted by the University of Michigan suggest that a dog's memory lasts only approximately five minutes.

No, not lawyers—we're talking about *ticks!* The problem isn't so much that they suck your dog's blood (really, how much can they drink?) as that they transmit diseases while drinking away. Ticks may first appear as tiny, dark, flat dots or as fat, blood-engorged tags hanging off your pet's skin. They can show up anywhere on your dog, but often inside the ears or on the legs. They're bad news, but here's what you can do:

o Keep tick spray on hand, and spray a small amount on a clean cloth or cotton ball. Dab it on and around the area where the tick is.

o After a few seconds, the tick should start to back out.

o If you don't have tick spray on hand, use alcohol or mineral oil.

o Flush the tick down the toilet.

o Apply rubbing alcohol to the area where the tick was attached.

WARNING: Never pull a tick out of a dog's skin while the tick's head is still buried. This could cause an infection.

Pawshake Cake

Reminder: Your dog wants you to know
he technically has seven birthdays each year (hint, hint).

o **Makes two 8-inch salivating celebration cakes** o

Your pup will roll over (or sit up or fetch the paper or be nice to the cat or stay off the couch) for a chance to sink his chops into a piece of Pawshake Cake. Our pup Biscuit says, "I'll shake to that."

2 cups whole wheat flour
2 teaspoons baking powder
½ cup honey
⅓ cup unsalted peanut butter
1 large egg
1 cup skim milk
¼ cup chopped unsalted peanuts

Preheat the oven to 350°F. Grease two 8- or 9-inch round cake pans with nonstick vegetable spray and dust with flour.

Stir together the flour and baking powder in a bowl and set aside. In a large bowl, cream together the honey and peanut butter with an electric mixer or wooden spoon. Beat in the egg and milk. Add the dry ingredients to the wet ingredients and mix until smooth.

Pour the batter into the cake pans. Sprinkle the top of the batter with the peanuts. Bake for 25 to 35 minutes, or until a toothpick inserted in the center of the cakes comes out clean.

Cool to room temperature before slicing and serving.

Store in an airtight container for up to 3 days, or wrap well and freeze for up to 2 months. (Thaw before serving.)

SALIVATIN' SERVING SUGGESTION: The cakes can be frosted, either singly or as a layer cake. See page 89 for a frosting recipe.

Holidogs

To err is human. To forgive, canine.

—Unknown

If there are no dogs in Heaven, then when I die I want to go where they went.

—Unknown

*H*olidays are always a time for *rrrr*eflection—a time to be thankful and remember all the good things that touch us. We can hardly think of anything we're more grateful for than the dogs and other animals who bless, enrich, and complete our lives. We know you understand that—or you wouldn't be holding this book in your two paws. May these recipes make your happy holidays even happier ones!

Peanut Butter Training Bites

A well-trained dog helps make the holidays bearable—almost.

◦ **Makes approximately 2 cups of sit-up-and-beg training bites** ◦

ROLL

OVER

GASP

FINISH

Same Time, Same Place

Housebreaking Tip: Puppy tummies are too small to hold their required daily nutrients in one feeding. They need to be fed three or four small meals throughout the day, then brought outside immediately after eating. Stay as consistent as possible with your puppy's feeding schedule. Establish a routine for feeding—same place, same time. This will help your new buddy to "learn the ropes" and can cut housebreaking time in half.

The fur can really fly around the holidays. Lots of parties, late hours, traveling—and, of course, the stress that comes with it all. Now imagine having a rowdy, couch-chewing, trash-shredding, barking holy terrier on your hands, too. And no, we're not talking about your husband. All your furry, four-legged kids will be "sitting pretty" all through the holidays if you use these tasty tidbits as their reward.

2 cups all-purpose flour
½ cup whole wheat flour
1 teaspoon molasses
2 tablespoons unsalted peanut butter
2 tablespoons canola oil

THRU

Preheat the oven to 350°F.

Stir together the flours in a bowl and set aside. Cream together the molasses, peanut butter, and oil in a large bowl. Add ½ cup water to the molasses mixture and mix well. Add the dry ingredients to the wet ingredients and mix until smooth.

Divide the dough into golf ball–size pieces and roll each into a log the diameter of training bites, typically ½ inch. Slice the logs into ⅛-inch-thick disks. Arrange on two ungreased baking sheets, and bake approximately 30 minutes, until golden brown and crunchy.

Cool completely before serving.

Store in an airtight container for up to 2 weeks, or wrap well and freeze for up to 2 months. (Thaw before serving.)

UNDER

Accidents Will Happen

If your dog has an accident in the house, 99.9 percent of the time it can be traced back to the fault of the human, not the dog. If you come home and discover an accident, chalk it up to experience and let it go with the resolve to make sure you let your dog out before you leave home next time. Never hit your dog for having an accident in the house.

Hitting your dog or angrily screaming does not and will not train her. Dogs (and humans) don't learn well under those circumstances. Instead of learning what you want, your dog may just learn to fear you without ever understanding what it is that you want her to do. Remember, your dog wants to please and understand you. She will learn much faster and more easily with positive reinforcement. Petting, happy-sounding praise words, treats, and love will train your dog better than anything.

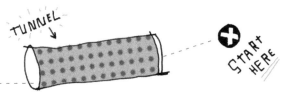

TUNNEL

START HERE

Holidogs

Vegetable Training Bites

○ Makes approximately 2 cups of stay-and-smile training bites ○

2 cups all-purpose flour
½ cup whole wheat flour
¼ cup minced carrots
¼ cup minced fresh parsley
1 teaspoon dried oregano
1 teaspoon molasses
2 tablespoons canola oil

Preheat the oven to 350°F.

Stir together the flours, carrots, parsley, and oregano in a bowl and set aside. In a large bowl, whisk together the molasses and oil. Add ½ cup water and mix well. Add the dry ingredients to the wet ingredients and mix until smooth.

Divide the dough into golf ball–size pieces and roll each into a log the diameter of training bites, typically ½ inch. Slice the logs into ⅛-inch-thick disks. Arrange on two ungreased baking sheets, and bake approximately 30 minutes, until golden brown and crunchy.

Cool completely before serving.

Store in an airtight container for up to 2 weeks, or wrap well and freeze for up to 2 months. (Thaw before serving.)

 Talk to the Hand!

When training your dog, use hand signals *at the same time* you use verbal commands. Why?

○ **It can be a life-saver in a situation where your dog can see but not hear you (or vice versa).**

○ **It gives you an extra option if your dog loses either sight or hearing in old age.**

And for some of us, it gives our dogs *two* ways to ignore us!

Cupid's Crush Cookies

Add a little spice to your dog's love life
with a fresh-baked Valentine.

o **Makes approximately 3 dozen cold-nose, warm-heart cookies** o

The licking, the panting, the rolling around on the carpet—and that's just Claire, our Great Dane, trying to get comfortable on the living room floor. These fetching love bites are guaranteed to put a twinkle in the eye of your lovestruck Labrador or lusty little Lhasa on St. Valentine's Day.

2 cups all-purpose flour
1 teaspoon baking powder
¼ teaspoon ground cinnamon
¼ teaspoon ground ginger
⅓ cup canola oil
½ cup molasses
2 tablespoons honey
¼ cup unsweetened applesauce
5 large egg whites
2 teaspoons pure vanilla extract

Preheat the oven to 350°F. Grease 2 baking sheets with nonstick vegetable spray.

Stir together the flour, baking powder, cinnamon, and ginger in a bowl and set aside. In a large bowl, stir together the oil, molasses, and honey until well mixed. Add the applesauce, egg whites, and vanilla to the molasses mixture and stir to blend. Add the dry ingredients to the wet ingredients and mix until smooth.

Drop the dough by the rounded teaspoonful, 1½ inches apart, on the baking sheets. Using the back of a spoon, press down on each dough drop to make an indention. Bake for 12 to 14 minutes, or until light golden.

Cool to room temperature before serving.

Store in an airtight container for up to 1 week, or wrap well and freeze for up to 2 months. (Thaw before serving.)

Holidogs

St. Puptrick's Emerald Isles

Aye, Lassie—now we know why Irish setter's eyes are smilin'.

○ Makes about 16 *lick*-of-the-Irish bites ○

Dogs Don't Have Heart Attacks!

Since fatty deposits typically don't form in a dog's arteries as they do in our own, dogs typically don't have heart attacks. Cholesterol isn't a problem for them, either. However, dogs *can* have high cholesterol levels, though that's usually a symptom of another ailment, such as liver disease, and doesn't lead to heart disease.

'Tis a top-of-the-mornin' recipe so easy to make you'll have the rest of the afternoon to yourself. Add a wee bit of chopped spinach, and these bites will be green as Ireland. Bake extra for all the dogs in the clan—and for the inner Irish wolfhound in all of us. We have a hunch you'll soon be Dublin it!

4 cups all-purpose flour
1 teaspoon baking powder
⅓ cup canola oil
1 teaspoon honey
⅓ cup finely chopped fresh spinach
Skim milk for brushing tops

Stir together the flour and baking powder in a bowl. Add the oil and mix with a fork until it is evenly distributed. Add 1 cup room tempera-

ture water, the honey, and the spinach, and work into a soft dough with a spoon. Then turn out onto a floured surface and knead with your hands.

Let the dough "relax" for 10 minutes (and you can relax, too).

Preheat the oven to 350°F.

Divide the dough in half, then divide those pieces in half. Keep going this way until you have 16 pieces. Roll the dough pieces into oval shapes about 3 inches long and 2 inches wide. Brush with milk and dust with flour.

Place the bites on a lightly greased and floured baking sheet and press your thumb lightly in the center of each oval. Bake for 20 minutes, or until light golden.

Cool to room temperature before serving.

Store in an airtight container for up to 5 days, or wrap well and freeze for up to 2 months. (Thaw before serving.)

Remember: Safety First

Always, *always* approach an injured dog with extreme caution—yes, *even* if it's your own trusted pet and *even* if it's showing signs of complete submission. A dog in pain may suddenly become aggressive. Don't make sudden gestures or loud noises. Speak in a soothing tone of voice. Be on guard for warning signs like growling, exposed teeth, raised hackles— even a seemingly submissive dog may strike out in fear or pain.

The Horrors of Heartworm

Heartworm is carried from dog to dog and throughout the entire dog neighborhood by mosquitoes. Heartworms live *in* a dog's heart and, if left untreated, lead ultimately to total heart failure—and often the symptoms don't show up for a couple of years. The *true* horror is that it's so easily prevented! Make sure all your dogs are on a once-a-month heartworm preventive year round.

Passover Pawtato Knishes

Taste-tempting tidbits too tasty to pass over!

○ Makes approximately 40 mini-knishes, enough for the whole synadog ○

They're Jewish! They're chewish! Your dog will never kvetch about his snacks again! Turns snack time into a *bone*-i-fide celebration—from Bark Mitzvahs to your next casual Tal*mutt* reading. *Mutt*sel Tov—and happy noshing!

Paw Pedicures

Examine your dog's feet regularly to inspect for wounds or cracking to the paws. Apply small amounts of petroleum jelly to your dog's paws to help keep pads soft and pliable and help soothe cracked and dry pads. Massage small amounts of petroleum jelly well into the pads.

3 potatoes, cooked and mashed (about 3 cups)
2 large eggs, beaten
¼ cup all-purpose flour
2 tablespoons canola oil
1 large egg yolk, beaten with 1 tablespoon water

Preheat the oven to 375°F. Grease a baking sheet with nonstick vegetable spray.

Stir together the potatoes, eggs, flour, and oil in a bowl. Using your hands, form balls the size of golf balls.

Place the balls on the baking sheet and brush with the egg yolk mixture. Bake for 15 to 20 minutes, or until golden brown.

Cool to room temperature before serving.

Store covered in the refrigerator for up to 3 days.

Easy on the Nails, Please

Hold up your dog's paw and look for the darker, shaded area of the nail, known as the quick. The nail can be cut safely and painlessly to approximately one-eighth of an inch in front of the quick. The quick is easier to find on a white nail than a black one. Cut cautiously! If you cut too far, not only will your pet *never* trust you again with the nail clippers, but you'll have a bloody mess on your hands. A styptic pencil or styptic powder generally works best on a cut, but if you don't have any available, apply corn starch—or even all-purpose flour—to the bleeding nail. Press it into the area firmly for a few minutes to stop the bleeding.

Water... Water... Must Have... Water...

To find out if your dog is dehydrated, pick up a fold of skin from around the middle of his back. If the skin stays up or returns to its position slowly, then your dog is dehydrated. If you can't get your dry doggy to drink water (maybe he's feeling under the weather), some fresh chicken, beef, or vegetable broth is often a tasty enticement. (Canned is fine, too, as long as it's sodium-free!)

Yappy Easter Hops

An eggstra special way to put some
"I love you" in your pup's Easter basset.

o **Makes 3 to 4 dozen eggscellent cookies** o

How Would *You* Like It?

**When housebreaking your dog, never push her
nose into her accidents. This is extremely de-
grading to your dog and can be deadly, too,
since dangerous bacteria may be present in her
waste. Use positive reinforcement by getting
her *outside* to begin with and then praising her
for going there.**

Your dogs will throw their paws in the air and bark, *"How*lelujah! They have risen!"* when these come out of the oven. Tasty enough to almost allow your dogs to forgive you for the photo session you made them sit through with the Easter Bunny.

3 cups all-purpose flour
1 teaspoon baking powder
½ teaspoon ground cinnamon
½ cup plain nonfat yogurt
½ cup molasses
2 large egg whites
1½ teaspoons pure vanilla extract

Preheat the oven to 350°F. Grease 2 baking sheets with nonstick vegetable spray.

Stir together the flour, baking powder, and cinnamon in a bowl and set aside. Whisk together the yogurt, molasses, egg whites, and vanilla in a large bowl. Add the dry ingredients to the wet ingredients and mix until smooth.

Drop the batter by the rounded teaspoonful, 1½ inches apart, on the baking sheets. Bake for 12 to 14 minutes, or until light golden.

Cool to room temperature before serving.

Store in an airtight container for up to 1 week, or wrap well and freeze for up to 2 months. (Thaw before serving.)

Cleanliness Is Next to Dogliness

Plastic dog dishes and water dishes are easily chewed and destroyed. When scratched and battered, they begin to harbor bacteria from small particles of food lodged in the scratches in the sides or bottom. Use heavy-bottom ceramic bowls or heavy-gauge stainless steel bowls to feed and water your dog.

Mutter's Day Barkin' Banana Bread

Mama dog will be more than happy to "heel" for a slice of this bread.

○ Makes 1 loaf of no-monkey-business banana-mama bread ○

At the end of the bed, you hear a noise—then up pop two ears and two big brown eyes. Who can resist? It's *Mutter*'s Day, and no matter how you slice it, this is today's *paw*fect way to loaf.

1¾ cups all-purpose flour
2 teaspoons baking powder
2 ripe bananas, mashed (to make 1 cup)
¼ cup molasses
⅓ cup canola oil
2 large eggs
1 apple, cored and diced (about 1 cup)

Preheat the oven to 350°F. Grease and flour an 8 X 4-inch loaf pan.

Stir together the flour and baking powder in a bowl and set aside. In a large bowl, beat together the bananas, molasses, oil, and eggs, adding the ingredients one at a time. Add the dry ingredients to the wet ingredients and stir until combined. Fold in the apple. Pour batter into the pan.

Bake for 1 hour, or until a toothpick inserted in the center of the loaf comes out clean.

Cool in the pan for 10 minutes, then turn out on a wire rack. Cool to room temperature before slicing and serving.

Store in an airtight container for up to 5 days, or wrap well and store in the freezer for up to 2 months. (Thaw before serving.)

I Can't Get a Word in Edgewise

A dog who barks excessively will drive you and your neighbors crazy. We have seen perfectly normal people do insane things to shut up a barking dog. Start training early. If your dog barks at strangers on your property, you may want to praise him for a few barks but then teach him a command like "Enough!" or "Quiet!" Yelling at your dog when he's barking won't do anything—he'll just think *you're* barking, too! Use positive reinforcement like love and treats to reward good behavior.

Plus She Can Just Forget about That Typing Job

Clip your dogs nails if you can hear "clicking" when she walks across a hard floor. Keeping your dog's nails well trimmed is an extremely important grooming and health tip. If left untrimmed, long curled nails can actually cripple dogs by growing into the pads of their paws.

Father's Day Muttigan Stew

Good . . . no, great to the last bite for
Mr. Hound-Around-Town on his big day.

○ **Makes 4 big-daddy, drool-inducing portions** ○

Ain't Misbehavin'

**It does no good to punish your dog after the
fact. If you don't catch your dog "in the act" of
misbehaving, she will not make the connection
between why she's being punished and what
she's done to deserve it. As common as it is for
us to think otherwise, dogs do *not* act up out of
spite or revenge. More than likely, if your dog
misbehaves, she is either bored or feeling anxiety about being separated from you, her pack
leader!**

He digs through the trash, shreds the
carpeting, and constantly jumps the
fence. Still, you gotta love him. This
snarf-it-up stew has all of his favorite
flavors in one devourable dish. Double it
and you'd have enough for dad and all
the little nippers to gorge on.

2 fresh tomatoes, finely chopped (about 1 cup)
1 large carrot, diced (about 1 cup)
4 sweet potatoes, diced (about 4 cups)
1 cup frozen peas
1 teaspoon honey
1 teaspoon ground sage
6 cups Homemade Chicken Stock (page 45), or
    canned, low-sodium chicken broth
2 cups diced cooked chicken

Combine the tomatoes, carrots, sweet potatoes, peas, honey, sage, and chicken stock in a large pot. Bring to a boil, then reduce to a simmer for 30 minutes. Add the chicken and simmer for 10 minutes.

Cool to room temperature before serving.

Serve with cooked rice (brown, preferably) or pasta (whole wheat, if possible).

Store in the refrigerator for up to 3 days.

 ## Say What You Mean, and Mean What You Say

Be consistent with your commands in communicating with your dog, especially a puppy in training. Keep commands simple and always use the same word to produce the desired result. If you mean "NO!" then don't say, "If you don't stop, I'm going to . . ." Say "NO!" To gain your dog's full attention, say his name first, before issuing a command.

Holidogs

Bark-B-Que Summer Day's Casserole

Summertime and the livin' is fleasy.

○ **Makes 8 pant-worthy portions for your hot dog to relish** ○

*Lab*or Day is the *paw*fect occasion for this vitamin-packed simmering summertime casserole. Dogs love sweet potatoes. In fact, they think they're yammy.

1 tablespoon canola oil
2 sweet potatoes, diced (about 2 cups)
1 cup finely chopped fresh broccoli or green beans
1 cup pearled barley
3 cups Homemade Chicken Stock (page 45), or canned, low-sodium chicken broth, or water, boiling
1 tablespoon ground sage
Bark-B-Qued Chicken (recipe follows)

Preheat the oven to 350°F.

Heat the oil in a Dutch oven or other flameproof covered casserole over medium heat. Add the sweet potatoes and broccoli and cook until lightly browned, about 10 minutes. Add the barley and cook for 1 minute. Add the boiling chicken stock and sage and cook for 3 to 4 minutes.

 But They Don't Need Sweat Socks

Dogs sweat through the pads of their feet, but their main method of dissipating heat for their entire body is through panting. In addition to making sure they have plenty of cool water to drink, you can help cool them down by providing a wading pool for them on very hot days.

Bake, covered, for 1 hour. Remove from the oven and add *Bark*-B-Qued Chicken.

Cool to room temperature before serving.

Store covered in the refrigerator for up to 3 days.

Bark-B-Qued Chicken

1 cup tomato sauce
½ teaspoon all-natural liquid smoke
1 tablespoon honey
4 ounces cooked boneless, skinless chicken, cut into bite-size pieces

Mix together the tomato sauce, liquid smoke, and honey in a large bowl. Place the chicken in the bowl and coat with the sauce.

 ## The Hazards of Heat Stroke

Never, *ever* leave your pet inside a parked car in hot weather—not even for a few minutes. The temperature inside a car with the windows rolled up enters the Death Zone in mere minutes. Even with the windows cracked the temperature can soar. People don't realize how shockingly fast a dog will perish—or how agonizing a death it is—suffocating inside a hot car. Some cities have stiff fines and penalties for leaving dogs unattended inside cars during summer months. Maybe jail time would help, too.

Great Pupkin Nut Bread

Calling all bloodhounds—here's a terrifying treat
for the spookiest night of the year.

○ Makes 6 frighteningly good miniloaves ○

Easy—and scary—to prepare even if you're a lazybones. Once your dogs try it, they'll drive you batty for more. You don't have to wait for *Howl*oween to enjoy this bewitching treat—they'll be *goblin* it down any day of the year.

1½ cups all-purpose flour
¾ teaspoon ground cinnamon
¼ teaspoon baking powder
Pinch of ginger
½ cup canola oil
¼ cup honey
One 18-ounce can pumpkin
2 large eggs

Them Ol' Bones

Many times aging dogs become bonier in certain areas of their bodies. Try to keep a soft pad, bed, or blankets available for an old dog to lie on to help soften the hard floor for those old bones. Special orthopedic bedding designed for older dogs is available at most pet stores.

Preheat the oven to 350°F. Grease and flour 6 aluminum mini bread pans.

Stir together the flour, cinnamon, baking powder, and ginger in a bowl and set aside. In a large bowl, stir together the oil and honey. Add the pumpkin and eggs, one at a time, and stir to combine. Stir in ¼ cup water. Add the dry ingredients to the wet ingredients and mix until smooth.

Fill the bread pans ⅔ full. Bake for 35 to 40 minutes, or until a toothpick inserted in the center of a loaf comes out clean.

Cool to room temperature before slicing and serving.

Store in an airtight container for up to 5 days, or wrap well and freeze for up to 2 months. (Thaw before serving.)

Idle Jaws Are the Devil's Workshop

A bored dog is a destructive dog! Keep a few sturdy, safe toys around for your dogs to chew on and play with. A safe chew toy satisfies your dog's natural tendency to chew and helps divert attention away from your treasured family heirlooms and personal possessions. Rotate toys in and out weekly to help prevent boredom.

Holidog Beast Feast

A serving so celebratory it turns every day into a hound holiday.

○ **Makes 8 or more beast feasts, depending on the size of your pup's tum** ○

The scent of sage and apples always reminds us of warming our paws on a cold autumn day, but this dish's full-bodied flavor warms the tummy, too. Simple to *paw*pare, it's a delicious combination of nutritious fruit, vegetables, and chicken and makes an extra special holiday meal—anytime of year.

But Do I Get My *AARF* Discount?

Older dogs may not absorb vitamins and minerals as readily as younger dogs can. Talk with your veterinarian to determine if your aging pet might benefit from additional dietary supplements.

1 small apple, diced (about ½ cup)
1 tablespoon canola oil
2 pounds boneless chicken, diced
½ cup unsweetened applesauce
1 teaspoon dried sage
1 cup frozen peas or green beans, thawed and
    drained
1 cup wild rice or long grain rice
3 cups Homemade Chicken Stock (page 45), or
    canned, low-sodium chicken broth

Preheat the oven to 350°F.

Sauté the apple in the oil for 2 minutes, or until tender. Place the apple in the bottom of Dutch oven or similar covered casserole. Add the remaining ingredients, stirring to combine.

Cover and bake for 1 hour, or until the rice is tender.

Cool to room temperature before serving. Store covered in the refrigerator for up to 3 days.

A Couch *Petato*

As your dog's aging bones and joints become stiff and achy, he'll be much more apt to plop down on his pillow and stay put for longer and longer periods of time. Be sure you keep the dog bed in a draft-free, comfy area, out of the hot sun.

Some older dogs suffering from arthritis and other joint disorders have shown dramatic improvement in mobility and pain reduction from glucosamine and chondroitin. Some antioxidant vitamins and minerals may play a role in keeping your dog healthy and active as he ages. Consult with your vet for his or her recommendations.

 ## You're Only as Old as You Feel

Dogs' dietary needs tend to change with age. A well-balanced diet lower in calories will help counter on older dog's less active lifestyle. A normal "senior" diet is lower in calories, fat, and protein and slightly higher in fiber. However, if your dog is healthy and active and maintaining a healthy weight, there may be no reason to switch to a "senior" diet.

Hanukkah Hound Honey Cake

We served the whole cake
and watched as our dog Torah hole in it.

○ **Makes enough to nosh on every night of Hanukkah** ○

Do I Look Like a Siberian Husky?

Be mindful of your canine's comfort in winter weather—when the mercury drops to bitter-cold levels, your dog is feeling it, too. Just because he's wearing a fur coat doesn't mean he can't feel miserable! The *least* damage cold will do is cause joint stiffness and aggravate arthritis; all too often it causes hypothermia and death. If you *must* leave your dog outside, change the water bowl often to prevent freezing—wintertime dehydration is all too common!

Attention, all ortho*dogs*! A recipe direct from *Chew*rusalem, with milk and honey, just like the old days. Light the menorah and dine by candlelight—this cake is heavenly!

1 cup all-purpose flour
1 teaspoon baking powder
1 teaspoon ground cinnamon
3 tablespoons carob powder (available at health food stores)
⅓ cup canola oil
¾ cup honey
2 large eggs
¾ cup skim milk
1 teaspoon pure vanilla extract

Preheat the oven to 350°F. Grease a 9-inch round cake pan with nonstick vegetable spray and dust with flour.

Stir together the flour, baking powder, cinnamon, and carob powder in a bowl and set aside. In a large bowl, whisk together the oil and honey. Add the eggs, one at a time, stirring to incorporate. Add the milk and vanilla, and combine. Add the dry ingredients to the wet ingredients and mix until smooth.

Spread the batter evenly in the cake pan. Bake for 25 to 30 minutes, or until a toothpick inserted in the center of the cake comes out clean.

Cool to room temperature before cutting and serving.

Store in an airtight container for 3 days, or wrap well and freeze for up to 2 months. (Thaw before serving.)

Give Antifreeze the Deep Freeze

Antifreeze is toxic to your dog. What's worse is that dogs are naturally attracted to its sweet, syrupy aroma and flavor. Even a tiny amount—a quick slurp from the driveway—can fatally poison your pooch. Keep antifreeze up and out of harm's way—for your dog's sake! To be on the safe side, buy antifreeze made from *propylene* glycol instead of the very toxic *ethylene* glycol. It's biodegradable, it's recyclable, and it's less harmful to the environment—not to mention our pets!

Holidogs

Santa Paws Holidog Cake

This year's season's grrrrreetings (and eatings)
to all the dogs on your list.

○ Makes 1 festive holi*dog* cake, enough to serve 6 to 8 furry elves ○

Fleas Navidad

Flea eggs incubate and hatch in rugs, furniture, cracks in the floor—practically anywhere. You can reduce or even eliminate your household's flea population by (I hate to say it) housework. If your dog has fleas, chances are your home does, too. Here's what you can do:

- **Thoroughly clean and vacuum your floors and carpeting often—at least once a week.**

- **Wash your dog's bedding at the same time.**

- **Bathe your dog with an all-natural flea shampoo, avoiding those with harsh chemicals. Ask your vet to suggest a good brand.**

Santa Paws knows who's been naughty and who's been nice. And he says all the dogs in your house deserve a slice (or two) of fresh-baked holi*dog* cheer! Guaranteed to put a festive, *fleas* navidad wiggle into all your hairy helpers.

2 cups whole wheat flour
¼ cup wheat germ
2 teaspoons baking powder
1 teaspoon ground cinnamon
¾ cup molasses
½ cup canola oil
2 large eggs
1 teaspoon pure vanilla extract
1 large apple, cored and diced

Preheat the oven to 350°F. Grease a 12-cup bundt pan with nonstick vegetable spray and flour.

Stir together the flour, wheat germ, baking powder, and cinnamon in a bowl and set aside. In a large bowl, whisk together the molasses and oil. Add the eggs, one at a time, whisking to blend. Add the vanilla and ½ cup water. Add the dry ingredients to the wet ingredients and mix until smooth. Fold in the apple.

Pour the batter into the bundt pan. Bake for 30 to 40 minutes, or until a toothpick inserted in the center of the cake comes out clean.

Cool to room temperature before slicing and serving.

Store in an airtight container for up to 3 days, or wrap well and store in the freezer for up to 2 months. (Thaw before serving.)

Of Course, That Doesn't Leave Much Time for Hobbies

An average flea lives three to four months and can produce thousands upon thousands of eggs during that time.

And just forget about quality time with the kids!

And You Thought It Just Kept Bugs Away from *You*

Look for citronella spray or oil to use as an all-natural aid in repelling fleas. It's a lot easier than training your dog to use the swatter. Trust us on this one.

New Year's Eve Midnight Licks

A grrrrreat way to start the New Year.

○ **Makes 40 floppy new ear cookies** ○

We aren't the world's biggest fans of black-eyed peas, a New Year's tradition for prosperity, but we felt certain that dogs would like their own tradition for, uh, *paws*perity? Just think of the carob chips as black-eyed peas. It's sure to bring you good "lick" all year long!

1 cup all-purpose flour
¼ cup whole wheat flour
½ teaspoon baking powder
¼ cup canola oil
1 large ripe banana, mashed
½ cup unsweetened applesauce
1 large egg
1 cup quick rolled oats
1 cup carob chips (available from health food stores)

Preheat the oven to 350°F. Grease 2 baking sheets with nonstick vegetable spray.

Stir together the flours and baking powder in a bowl and set aside. Beat the oil, banana, and applesauce together in a bowl using an electric mixer or a spoon. Beat in the egg. Add the dry ingredients to the wet ingredients and mix until smooth. Stir in the oats and carob chips.

Drop the dough by the rounded teaspoonful, 1½ inches apart, on the baking sheets. Bake for 8 to 10 minutes, until light golden.

Cool to room temperature before serving.

Store in an airtight container for up to 1 week, or wrap well and freeze for up to 2 months. (Thaw before serving.)

The Dog Who Came in from the Cold

Carefully wipe off your dog's paws after a winter walk. It only takes a minute, and it will clear the stinging salt and winter's dirty sludge out of the pads.

Of course, you *could* always get your dog some fashionable booties. . . .

Holidogs

Yorkie Pudding

It's a festive holi*dog* tradition, especially with the Yorkshire terrier set.
Now, where did you say you put the roast beef?

○ **Feeds at least 4 dozen Yorkies** ○

Pssst . . . Want an Investment Tip?

Make an appointment with your dog's veterinarian for a general checkup *every year*—the money it costs will be an investment in your *shared* future!

Special note: No Yorkies were harmed in the testing of this recipe. In medieval England, where this recipe originated, Yorkshire pudding was commonly used to fill travelers up at inns before the (expensive) meat was served. Today we just know it as a yummy dish from days of yore.

1 cup all-purpose flour
1 large egg
½ cup skim milk
2 to 3 tablespoons canola oil

Sift the flour into a bowl. In a separate bowl, beat the egg, then stir in the milk and ½ cup water. Slowly pour the egg mixture into the flour and whisk until the batter is smooth.

Let the batter rest for approximately 1 hour.

Place the oven rack in the top position, and preheat the oven to 425°F.

Divide the oil among 12 metal (not nonstick) muffin cups. Place the muffin pan on the top rack of the hot oven for 10 to 15 minutes (until the oil is very hot). Pour the rested batter into the muffin cups and place the pan back on the top rack of the oven. Bake for approximately 15 minutes, until the popovers are puffed and golden.

Cool completely before serving.

Store refrigerated in an airtight container for up to 3 days.

Great Reason to Have a Dog (as if you really needed one)

Those of us who share our lives with dogs live longer, have less stress, suffer less depression, and have fewer heart attacks. If you're feeling stressed and/or depressed even though you *have* a dog, just imagine how much worse it would be *without* one!

Index

About the Authors

MARK BECKLOFF and DAN DYE are the founders of Three Dog Bakery, the world's original bakery for dogs. They've been featured in numerous media venues, including the cover of *Forbes* magazine, *Oprah*, *Today*, *Late Night with Conan O'Brien*, *People*, the *New York Times*, and *USA TODAY*. The authors of three previous books, *Short Tails and Treats from Three Dog Bakery*, *Three Dog Bakery Cookbook*, and *Amazing Gracie*, they also hosted the Food Network show *Three Dog Bakery . . . Unleashed!* for two years. Mark and Dan currently reside in Tucson, Arizona, with their hounds: Dottie 2.0, Biscuit, Claire, and Lu.